HOW TO BEAT
PROCRASTINATION
IN THE
DIGITAL AGE

6 CHANGE PROGRAMS
FOR
6 PERSONALITY STYLES

Dr. Linda Sapadin

PsychWisdom Publishing
www.PsychWisdom.com
From the **NOW I GET IT!** Series

ISBN: 978-0-9836766-5-2

The individuals described in this book are composites of more than one
real person. The actions and statements ascribed to such individuals are
also a composite of the actions and statements of the persons on whom the
individual is based.

For additional resources, go to:
www.BeatProcrastinationCoach.com
www.PsychWisdom.com

Contact Dr. Sapadin at LSapadin@DrSapadin.com

Cover Design by Harvey Appelbaum

DEDICATED TO

Your Best Self

Nurture it and Sustain it

Let it be Your Guide to a Fabulous Future

Also by Dr. Linda Sapadin

Now I Get It! Totally Sensational Advice for Living and Loving. A collection of 62 empowering and entertaining columns on enhancing relationships, enriching communication skills and expanding personal growth. Outskirts Press 2007, Inkstone Press (Australia), 2008.

Master Your Fears: How to Triumph Over Your Worries and Get On With Your Life. John Wiley, 2004, also published in Korea.

It's About Time! The 6 Styles of Procrastination and How to Overcome Them. Viking and Penguin, 1996, also published in Japan.

Beat Procrastination and Make the Grade: The 6 Styles of Procrastination and How Students Can Overcome Them. Penguin, 1999 with Jack Maguire.

101 Great Ways to Improve Your Life. Chapter Title: *Overcoming Resistance: What's Stopping You?* Self-Growth, Inc. 2006

TABLE OF CONTENTS

Which Styles(s) Do You Relate To?

Personality Type	Thinking Style	Speaking Style	Acting Style	Emotional Need for
Perfectionist	Either/Or	I Should	Flawless	Control
Dreamer	Fuzzy	I Wish	Passive	Importance
Worrier	Anxious	What if?	Cautious	Safety
Crisis-Maker	Intense	Vivid	Climactic	Drama
Defier	Challenging	Quarrelsome	Resistant	Autonomy
Pleaser	Dutiful	Agreeable	Frazzled	Approval

CHAPTER 1

PROCRASTINATING
IN THE
DIGITAL AGE

PEOPLE HAVE STRUGGLED WITH procrastination since the beginning of time. Let's see, shall I spend the evening doing mindnumbing clean-up chores or enjoy a good time with my friends? Shall I do tedious and tiresome paperwork or plop down on the couch and watch a movie? It's never been easy to control our impulses and urges, especially when the "correct" choice goes against our grain.

In the modern world, however, procrastination is even harder to conquer. Accessible, appealing, addictive distractions are everywhere. Beepers beckon. Diversions call. Entertainment entices. Digital devices tempt. Social networks, gaming, blogging, texting, i-Pods, Podcasts, You Tube, websites, porn sites, chat rooms, video streaming—and more—seduce. Add up the hours you spend on stuff that has nothing to do with your personal or career goals. Now, is it any wonder that you're teetering on the edge of the Boulevard of Broken Dreams?

Though there were (and are) plenty of pre-digital ways to fritter away your time, digital temptations are just so much easier, enjoyable and seductive. Sure you could always neglect your chores to take a snooze or flip through a magazine or actually read a book. But how can you compare those distractions with the ones currently available to us?

You're uploading photos onto Facebook when a friend insists you check out a YouTube that has just gone viral. As you're watching the video, you get another text about an incredible new band. You listen to its music on Grooveshark, view the lead singer on Tumblr, join the band's fan page on Twitter. And even if you're not a member of the Facebook generation, you're still reading your e-mail, checking out a lead article on your home page, going online to view your financial investments and playing Solitaire. Before you know it, a few minutes have become a few hours; a few hours have become the better part of the day and you are left wondering—where *did* the day go?

Exciting, fast-paced entertainment has actually changed the way your brain operates. Your gray matter now craves excitement. If a task doesn't immediately hold your interest, your mind gravitates to other matters as your accomplishments gravitate downhill. Don't live one more day regretting how you spend your time. You deserve better. You can do better. This book will show you how. Let's begin with a basic understanding of the procrastination beast.

Procrastination: An Approach-Avoidance Conflict

We bandy around the word procrastination all the time. But what exactly is it? Some people believe it's nothing more than laziness. Sorry, not true. The crux of procrastination is that it's an unresolved "approach-avoidance" conflict. A part of you knows you need (or even want) to do a task but another part of you resists doing it. Like a Hamlet in the world of action, you're torn between two impulses: *"to do or not to do."* Such ambivalence makes it tough for you to choose a clear commitment to action. So what happens?

- You start doing the task, but lingering resistance means you work at a snail's pace.

- You stay stuck in your Hamlet-like conflict until you lurch into action at the last minute, prodded on by an impending deadline or a ticked-off third party.

- You put a lot of effort into the project but never complete it because you conclude that it's "not quite good enough."

- Or you never get beyond your crippling conflict. Your positive energy remains dammed, damning you to yet another setback.

Here's how Michael, a crisis-maker attorney and top notch procrastinator described his Hamlet-like conflict: "I have every intention of sitting down to work, but it's hard for me to focus on anything early on. It's not until I'm under the gun that my creative energies awaken. Then I'm on a roll. I work right through the night, finishing it just before deadline—though that doesn't count the times an unforeseen glitch occurs. In such situations, I rely on a Hail Mary pass, making up one excuse after another as to why my brief isn't ready on time—praying for a reprieve from an empathetic judge."

Memo to Michael: Football coaches only call for a Hail Mary when time is running out and they have no other option. This is a piss poor way to approach work responsibilities—especially since most Hail Marys fail in the stadium as they do in the real world.

Some people experience their Hamlet-like struggle as: *"should I work or should I play?"* Here's how Brett, a dreamer procrastinator, described his internal battle: "I could do it if I felt like it. The thing is—I never feel like it. I'm drawn to so many other activities that putting time into any work project takes a back seat. The major competition: Facebook and Twitter, video games, playing the guitar. I know I'm a creative person, but it's hard for me to stay on task. I'm so easily drawn to what feels like fun."

Still others experience their struggle as: *"should I stay or should I go?"* Here's how Deidre, a defier procrastinator, described her Hamlet-like conflict: "I want so badly to quit my miserable dead-end job.

I'd love to work for myself, be my own boss. But whenever there's a chance to figure out how I might start my own business, I say 'Screw it; I'll do it later.' So I'm stuck where I am and see no new prospects for my future."

Some attribute the cause of their procrastination to a learning disability or to ADD (attention deficit disorder). Or they believe that anxiety or depression prevents them from summoning up the energy to accomplish anything of value. Yes, it's possible that any of these diagnoses may augment your tendency to procrastinate. So address them. But don't hesitate to immerse yourself in the change programs in this book. Not only will they help you tame your tendency to procrastinate but they'll also help you with the above issues.

Finally, there are folks who believe that they've inherited a lazy gene. A simple explanation, but is it true? Not likely. It's more likely that you've got an abundance of energy for what you *want* to do but not for what you're *expected* to do. If you've developed a talent for avoiding activity that's not stimulating to you, challenge yourself to discover something interesting in the task—even if most of it is humdrum.

- In Marcel Proust's words, "The journey of discovery begins not with new vistas but with having new eyes with which to behold them."

- In Henry David Thoreau's words, "It's not what you look at that matters, it's what you see."

- Appreciate that life requires you to engage in struggles that you don't like in order to get to where you want to be. Read that sentence again. Imprint it on your brain. It's an important life lesson.

No matter what you believe is the cause of your procrastination, always remember that you are more than your label. Do not give up on yourself. Believe in what you can do. Work at what you must do.

Yes, it'll take time and effort. But so what? Your dream is worth it! *You're* worth it!

Maybe You're On the Wrong Track?

Will Rogers, born in 1879, was a Cherokee Indian, a cowboy noted for his roping skills, a movie star, a columnist, and today, a legend. He was one smart guy but no boring intellectual. He spoke in simple words that everyone could understand:

> *"Even if you're on the right track,*
> *you'll get run over if you just sit there."*

Are you sitting on the right track watching your dreams fade into obscurity? Or could it be that your procrastination is a sign that you're on the wrong track? Think about it.

- Do you feel bummed out at work, yet know you'd thrive in another career better suited to your interests and inclinations?

- Do you believe that your work environment is stifling, yet know that you'd flourish in an environment with a more nurturing culture?

- Do you feel your troubled relationship is draining your energy, yet know that if you could just work out a few kinks in the relationship, you'd feel so much better?

If you're on the wrong track, do consider making a change. Not an impulsive, "I'm outta here" change, but a well-thought-out change that both your head and your heart approve of. If, however, you're on the right track but just sitting there doing squat, it's time for you to explore the inner dynamics of your procrastination. It's likely:

- *You feel helpless, powerless, and frustrated.* You may direct this feeling inward and come to regard yourself as incompetent.

Or, direct this feeling outward in the form of anger with other people or with your situation.

- *You rationalize your lack of action, believing that there's nothing much you can do about it.* You say things like, "I'm just lazy by nature." Or make self-vindicating statements like, "Sorry, I *always* forget to return calls." Or you may forestall criticism by laughing at or even boasting about your procrastination, ignoring what's at stake for you. You may act as if your tendency to procrastinate is a fact of life as immutable as eye color rather than an acquired habit, capable of being modified.

- *You obsess about what you're putting off, but still don't take action.* Obsessing may initially feel productive, but then you realize it's like a dog chasing its tail—going round and round, getting nowhere fast. You may obsess about what will happen if you don't act—failure, humiliation, regret. But does the obsessing change anything? An emphatic no! Indeed, it may only make things worse as it drains your positive energy.

- *You feel recurring regret that eats away at your capacity to attain what you want.* Such regret often escalates into crippling guilt and humiliating shame that makes altering your pattern seem ever more difficult.

"*Regrets, I've had a few, too few to mention,*" crooned Sinatra. If your regrets are too few to mention, you're lucky! However, keep dragging your feet rather than putting in the effort to make your life work and your regrets will be too many to mention. Over time, such regrets will close windows of opportunity, undermine your confidence and give rise to negative energy that will derail you from ever reaching your goals.

A few examples:

- John lost his good credit rating for neglecting to pay his credit card bills on time.

- Allison lost an opportunity for promotion by failing to attend career advancement seminars.

- Maria almost lost her life. No exaggeration, some procrastination can truly be fatal.

Here's Maria's story: Maria knew for months that she had what she called "a funny spot" on her breast. She was so nervous about it that she only told her best friend. Her friend encouraged her to get it checked out. Maria was always "meaning to go" but was afraid that "they might find something wrong." Tragically, something was wrong. By the time she went for an exam, her cancer was far more advanced than it was when she first noticed it. Maria regrets what she calls her "stupidity." She knows her behavior made no sense. But she also knows that it's not unusual for *emotion to trump reason*.

Of course, procrastination doesn't usually yield such dire consequences. However, it still has its costs, not only making it more difficult to strive toward personal goals but even to formulate them. Those who tend to dawdle and delay often gripe about "not knowing who I am, what I want or how to get it." They become demoralized when they see others rack up success after success, while they're still stuck cleaning up the residue of their procrastination.

Here's David's story: David used to brag about making his first million before he turned 30. Nowadays, he's lost faith in himself. Watching his friends obtain high-paying jobs while he's still struggling to finish his incompletes in college isn't exactly a recipe for self-confidence. David's worrying is justified. Though he started out as astute as his friends, he's not keeping up with them. He's learning an important lesson the hard way: *no matter how high your potential is, if you don't act on that potential, you'll become less competent over time.*

The Emotional Toll of Procrastination

Procrastination is the gift that keeps on giving and giving—not only rationalizations and regrets but also distressing emotions, such as:

- *Panic*—At any stage of a task, you may be overwhelmed by panic or what I call the "Oh, my God!" syndrome. You may panic about whether you have the capability to handle what's expected of you, whether you'll fall so far behind that you won't ever catch up, or whether you'll go loco over your lackluster performance. Even after you've completed a task, you may still taste the bitter residue of panic as you agonize over the quality of your work and what it says about you and your future.

- *Discouragement*—In contrast to the red-hot frenzy of panic, discouragement is the desolate, disheartening ebb state. Riding the endless roller coaster of hysterical highs and discouraging lows can leave you feeling exhausted. As you confront your disappointment in yourself, you may be tempted to give up. Sad to say, you may yield to this temptation without any real need to do so. Quitting is easy; figuring out the best path for you, then working hard to make it happen is tough.

- *Depression*—The hallmark signs of depression are feelings of helplessness and hopelessness, often expressed as: "I can't do it; no use even trying; it's all too much; I'm giving up." Of course, anyone can have down days. If talking with friends or getting a good night's sleep revives your motivation, there may be nothing much to worry about. But if depression hangs on, don't ignore it. Procrastination may be triggering your depression or depression may be triggering your procrastination. Either way, consult a psychologist to determine how to address those feelings.

- *Denial*—Some procrastinators defend their stalling tactics by calling them "creative." It's good to procrastinate, they claim. Why do things on time when you can put them off till later? It's amazing how some people can fool themselves about almost anything. If you're tempted to spin your procrastination into a laudable trait, don't. If there's one thing you owe yourself, it's honesty. But aren't there *ever* good reasons to put things off? Absolutely! Here are three:

You're Overcommitted: You're juggling so many balls that you just can't handle one more and do justice to it. If that's true, be honest about your predicament—both with yourself and with others. Rather than simply procrastinate (say you'll get to it but don't), create a time in the future when you won't be spread so thin. At that point, you'll be more motivated to do a better job.

You're Overemotional: When your emotions are riding high, it's not the best time to take care of many matters. In the heat of anger, fear, hurt, even joy, it's easy to regret your actions. So yes, postpone making a serious commitment when your emotions are soaring. When you've calmed down, consult both your head and your heart to decide the best path to take.

You're Impulsive: We're a fast-paced society. We're impatient. We want things to be done, fixed, completed right away. The more technologically sophisticated we are, the faster we expect things to happen. Yet acting impulsively (like tweeting without thinking) is often a precursor to kicking yourself the next day. There's a huge difference between being so laid back that you don't act when you should and taking the time to tackle your tasks responsibly.

> *"The greatest of faults, I should say,*
> *is to be conscious of none."*
> ~ **Thomas Carlyle**

How Extensive Is Your Procrastination Pattern?

People aren't perfect. Procrastination happens. A messy closet remains that way, even though you promised yourself you'd get to it. A tough talk is delayed until you have no choice. A response to a request falls through the cracks. For many, however, procrastination is not something that happens on occasion; it's *a chronic, pervasive and deeply rooted pattern.* If you are one of these people, you know you have a built-in tendency to let things slide—not only with challenging tasks but even with simple ones. To discover how pervasive your procrastination problem is, answer the following questions. Respond "Yes" if you often or frequently do what's described or "No" if you rarely or never do it.

1. Do I put things off that jeopardize my career, wealth, health, or relationships?

2. Do I delay doing things until a crisis develops?

3. Do I hesitate to take action because I fear change?

4. Do I think a lot about stuff I'd like to do but rarely get them off the ground?

5. Do I think I'm special, hence don't need to do the boring, tedious work that others do?

6. Do I commit myself to so many obligations that I can't find time to attend to all of them?

7. Do I leave tasks unfinished, jumping from one to another without completing any?

8. Does surfing the Web, gaming or watching a reality show become more compelling to me when I seek to avoid doing what I know I need to do?

9. Do I put off tackling a job until I can find the "best" time to do it?

10. Do I tell myself "I've got to change the way I do things" but somehow never get around to making even a little change?

11. Do I joke around saying there's "no time like tomorrow" to do whatever needs to be done today?

12. Do I justify my procrastination by giving stock responses, such as: "I work best under pressure; I don't have time; I'm waiting to be inspired?"

How many "Yes" responses did you have? The more you have, the more pervasive is your procrastination problem. How frustrating is that? Not only for you but for those who live and work with you. But lucky you, all that is about to change. Keep on reading!

One Size Does Not Fit All

As you might have guessed from taking the quiz, all procrastination styles are not the same. If you've tried to curtail your pattern but haven't been successful, it could be that you haven't found the right approach. If it were a simple matter, like "making resolutions " or "just doing it," don't you think your mom's nagging or your teacher's scolding would have cured you of it years ago? Most how-to advice highlights developing better organizational skills and increased discipline. Those are good skills to learn; but they're not enough. Why not? Because many habits—including procrastination—*are driven by subconscious personality traits and emotional needs.*

An analogy: If you wish to lose weight yet know little about nutrition, it's a good idea to learn about calories, fat content, food groups, etc. However, if you're so knowledgeable in that area that you could teach a course on nutrition, yet you're still overweight, your failure and frustration has nothing to do with knowledge and everything to do with personality traits and emotional needs.

- Perhaps you have low frustration tolerance, hence you satisfy your impulse to eat the moment you feel a bit hungry, discouraged or dissatisfied.

- Perhaps you long to fit into the social scene, hence if your friends are having pizza, *that's* what you're having too.

- Perhaps you make promises to yourself that are destined to fail because you make them when you're in one physical state (stuffed), ignoring how you'll feel when you're in another physical state (starved).

Whatever self-defeating pattern of behavior you want to conquer, you must know your personality style. This is essential, as the right advice for one style is the wrong advice for another. One change program does not fit all. Two examples:

If your procrastination is driven by *a perpetual pursuit of perfection*, it's essential that you pay *less* attention to details. Putting too much emphasis on the details inhibits your ability to complete your work. Why? Because if you believe your work isn't perfect, you'll never want to wrap it up and call it a day.

However, if your procrastination is driven by *a perpetual pursuit of pie-in-the-sky dreams*, it's essential that you pay *more* attention to details. Not enough emphasis on the details will thwart your progress.

Why? Because though you may have spectacular ideas, if you neglect doing important details, your ideas will never see the light of day.

Because procrastination is *not* fueled by the same reasons, I describe 6 personality styles and provide you with a change program tailor-made for *each* style. The change programs are *not* designed to turn you into a rigid, clock-driven, no-fun person. The opposite, however, is also true. I'm not suggesting you live the life of an unstructured, spur-of-the-moment, follow-your-impulse person. You may question: Why not? Why can't I live in the moment, doing only what I feel like doing? The short answer: Because a funny thing happens when you're working at a job, involved in a relationship or simply trying to create a life for yourself. People expect you to take care of responsibilities. And when you don't, when you're late or when you do a half-assed job, stuff happens. Unpleasant stuff! So what's the goal?

In one word:

BALANCE

And, if there's one thing that can throw you off balance, it's procrastination. With so many seductive distractions, it's tough to maintain a balanced life in the digital age. And yet, you can break the pattern. Indeed, *you need to break the pattern*. For the consequences become increasingly severe as time goes on.

- You talk your way into a dream job—only to be fired when they notice your less than sterling work habits.

- You have bills to pay—only you delay doing it and next thing you know the collection agency is on your back.

- You have every intention of revising your resume—only you neglect to do so and are still stuck in a boring dead-end job.

- You want to feel closer to that special someone—only you put off addressing the conflicts and now the relationship is in jeopardy.

Yes, procrastination can have many negative unforeseen effects. So, kudos to you for deciding to squash your debilitating habit before it squashes your future.

In the next chapter, you will find a self-assessment quiz to help you determine which of the six styles is yours. Know that each style has its splendid strengths and its wavering weaknesses. The goal of each change program is *not* to change you into another type of personality. That would be counterproductive and frankly, rather insulting. Yes, it might be helpful if you were better organized like your sibling or more detail oriented like your friend—but you've got admirable traits that they don't have. Whatever your style, there's no need for a personality makeover; the change program for each style works *with* you—helping you to nurture and sustain your best self.

CHAPTER 2

SIX PERSONALITY STYLES
A SELF-ASSESSMENT QUIZ

Directions:

Complete each of the six quizzes as follows:

Reflect on each question as honestly as you can. Then, write in the box the number that best portrays your personality.

1 = Not typically me.

2 = Sometimes, this is me.

3 = Yup, that's definitely me.

After completing all the questions in each quiz, add up your score for that style.

Style 1 Quiz

Write in the box the number that best describes your personality style.

 1 = Not typically me.

 2 = Sometimes, this is me.

 3 = Yup, that's definitely me.

		1, 2 or 3
1.	Do I have a "black or white" mentality, paying scant attention to the gray area in between?	
2.	Do tasks often take me longer to do because whatever I do I want it to be "just right?"	
3.	Do I have difficulty starting or completing a project because my standards are so high that I intimidate myself?	
4.	Am I reluctant to delegate tasks or get involved in a group project unless others do things my way?	
5.	Do others see me as being rigid, inflexible or finicky?	
6.	Am I often critical of the quality of my work or disappointed by how long it took me to complete it?	
7.	Am I satisfied with what I do only if it is as good as it could possibly be?	
8.	Do I look upon my failures as embarrassments that I don't like to have revealed?	
9.	Do I have difficulty maintaining a sense of humor while struggling to do a task I'm not skilled at?	
10.	Do I get preoccupied with details, rules, or schedules that others don't seem to care much about?	

Total Score for STYLE 1 _____

Style 2 Quiz

Write in the box the number that best describes your personality style.

1 = Not typically me.

2 = Sometimes, this is me.

3 = Yup, that's definitely me.

	1, 2 or 3
1. Do I think a lot about what I'd like to accomplish but rarely get projects off the ground?	
2. Do I wait for opportunities to drop into my lap rather than take an active, "go get 'em" approach?	
3. Do I frequently let time drift by with passive activities like daydreaming, watching TV or casually surfing the Web?	
4. Do I spend more time thinking about the finished project than about doing the details I must do to make it happen?	
5. Do I long to be able to go from A to Z without having to deal with all those bothersome details in between?	
6. Do I wish someone else would handle the annoying details of life, freeing me to be more creative and do what I want to do?	
7. Do I find myself saying phrases like, "I'll try to..." or "Someday I will...?"	
8. Have others accused me of having my head in the clouds or being impractical about a matter?	
9. Do I tend to live in the moment, putting previous plans and priorities on the back burner?	
10. Do I expect great things from myself, then wonder why they don't seem to happen?	

Total Score for STYLE 2 _____

Style 3 Quiz

Write in the box the number that best describes your personality style.

1 = Not typically me.

2 = Sometimes, this is me.

3 = Yup, that's definitely me.

	1, 2 or 3
1. Do I hesitate to leave my comfort zone, avoiding situations that might make me feel anxious?	
2. Do I have difficulty making decisions, frequently vacillating about what I should do?	
3. Do I often seek assurance from others before I can start to work on a project?	
4. Do I have trouble completing work because I doubt my own judgment or don't trust my abilities?	
5. Do I feel worried about whether I can measure up to what others expect of me?	
6. Do I become uptight when an unexpected event disrupts my typical routine?	
7. Do I avoid uncomfortable situations by retreating to my digital gizmos?	
8. Do I tend to paralyze myself by worrying about the "what ifs" of life?"	
9. Do I maximize problems that might arise while minimizing my ability to deal with such problems?	
10. Do I believe I could achieve much more if only somebody would take me by the hand and show me the way?	

Total Score for STYLE 3 _____

Style 4 Quiz

Write in the box the number that best describes your personality style.

1 = Not typically me.

2 = Sometimes, this is me.

3 = Yup, that's definitely me.

		1, 2 or 3
1.	Do I put off taking care of tasks then, at the last minute, work frantically to get them done?	
2.	Do I feel that my life is a whirlwind and I'm never quite sure what the next day will bring?	
3.	Do my moods tend to change quickly and dramatically?	
4.	Do I get easily frustrated and show it by displaying anger or impulsively quitting?	
5.	Do I act in ways that other people find provocative, seductive, or attention getting?	
6.	Am I easily seduced into responding to my need of the moment?	
7.	Do I enjoy taking risks and love the thrill of living on the edge?	
8.	Do I have a tendency to get involved with a project, then abruptly detach myself and move on to something else?	
9.	Do I think of my life as so dramatic that it could be made into a soap opera?	
10.	Do I have little patience for activities that are slow, predictable or safe—preferring instead quick, action-oriented projects?	

Total Score for STYLE 4 _____

Style 5 Quiz

Write in the box the number that best describes your personality style.

1 = Not typically me.

2 = Sometimes, this is me.

3 = Yup, that's definitely me.

		1, 2 or 3
1.	Do I tend to criticize or ridicule people who are in authority?	
2.	Do I work slowly or ineffectively in order to sabotage a chore I resent doing?	
3.	Do I feel manipulated when I wind up having to do a task I don't want to do?	
4.	Do I feel that others often make unreasonable demands on me?	
5.	Do I blow off attending to chores by shrugging my shoulders and claiming I've forgotten to do them?	
6.	When people ask me why I did (or didn't do) something, do I view them as hassling or nagging me?	
7.	Do I believe that I'm doing a better job than others think or say I'm doing?	
8.	Do I take offense when others tell me how I could do things differently?	
9.	Do others get annoyed with me for failing to do my share of the work in a timely manner?	
10.	Do I become sulky, sarcastic, or argumentative when expected to do a task I dislike?	

Total Score for STYLE 5 _____

Style 6 Quiz

Write in the box the number that best describes your personality style.

1 = Not typically me.

2 = Sometimes, this is me.

3 = Yup, that's definitely me.

		1, 2 or 3
1.	Do I find it difficult to say "no" to people who ask for help, yet feel overburdened later on?	
2.	Do I have a strong need for approval from others?	
3.	When I'm involved in a project, do I find myself wondering, "How did I get into this?"	
4.	Do I feel weighed down by my lack of time and my busy workload?	
5.	When I get unexpected free time, do I start new projects instead of finishing up old ones?	
6.	Do I hate to ask anyone for help, afraid of what they'll think of me?	
7.	Do I get over-involved in other people's problems, postponing attention to my own?	
8.	Do I often complain that "I have no time," "I've too much to do," "I'm sooo busy?"	
9.	Do I run around doing a million things, yet often feel that I haven't accomplished much?	
10.	Do I enjoy being busy, but secretly think that maybe I don't know any other way to be?	

Total Score for STYLE 6 _____

My Major And Minor Styles

Now that you've finished all six quizzes, complete this final section as follows:

- In the column marked *Total Score,* write your total score for each individual quiz.

- In the column marked *Rank Order,* rank order your styles: #1 will be your highest total score, #2 the next highest and so on. Identical scores receive the same rank order.

- *Major styles* are those in which you received a score of 25 or more, *minor styles* a score of 15–24.

Personality Style	Total Score	Rank Order
I. Perfectionist		
2. Dreamer		
3. Worrier		
4. Crisis-Maker		
5. Defier		
6. Pleaser		

Any surprises? It could be that your results simply reinforce what you already knew. Or, you may be completely surprised. We don't always know ourselves as well as we think we do. What follows is a brief description of each style, along with its hallmark "But" excuse.

The Six Personality Styles

1. The Perfectionist: *"...BUT it's not perfect!"*

As a perfectionist, you find it difficult to complete a task because you don't want to do anything less than a perfect job. You may be concerned about satisfying your own high standards and/or the high expectations that you believe others have of you. Once you've started a task, you may spend far more time and energy working on it than is needed. Overworking, paradoxically, is an unrecognized form of procrastination. Though you may work hard, you don't always work smart.

2. **The Dreamer: "...*BUT I hate dealing with those annoying details!*"**
As a dreamer, you're adept at championing creative ideas but turning these ideas into full blown realities is your Waterloo. Soaring thinking without ground level doing leads to disappointing results. "It's hard to do" easily morphs into "It's too tough to do." Uncomfortable with the practical world, you may retreat into whimsical ways to obtain success, such as winning the lottery or somehow, someday getting a lucky break.

3. **The Worrier: "...*BUT I'm afraid to make a change!*"**
As a worrier, you hesitate to leave your comfort zone. You proceed through life with caution, worrying about 'what might happen if'. Confronting change and dealing with risk are challenging for you, hence you find it tough to make decisions. Even after you've made a decision, you tend to second guess it. Maximizing the difficulty of a problem while minimizing your ability to cope with it, erodes your self-confidence.

4. **The Crisis-Maker: "...*BUT I work best under pressure!*"**
As a crisis-maker, you crave living on the edge. Addicted to the rush of high emotion, imminent danger, and emergency activity, you delight in pulling things off at the final moment. Though rising to the occasion of a last minute crisis may initially feel victorious, it does get tiring. Despite staying up all night to work on your presentation, you know it wasn't as effective as it could have been had you put more time into it.

5. The Defier: "...*BUT why should I have to do it?*"

As a defier, you may be either openly rebellious, passive-aggressive or a combination of the two. If you have an openly rebellious style, you directly defy authority. Procrastination is one way to do this, as it lets you set your own time schedule one that no one else can control. As a passive-aggressive procrastinator, you're less blatant with your defiance. You simply say you'll do things, but don't. Both types of defiers tend to view routine tasks as impositions on their time, rather than as responsibilities to take in stride.

6. The Pleaser (Overdoer): "...*BUT I have so much to do!*"

As a pleaser, you find it hard to say "no" to others; hence your own needs often end up at the bottom of the pile. With so much to do, you feel frazzled by the lack of time, frenzied with your countless commitments. Since it's tough for you to refuse requests, procrastination becomes your indirect way of saying "no." You've yet to master the skills of creating priorities, establishing boundaries and setting limits, which makes you a prime candidate for early burnout.

If you related to more than one style of procrastination, don't panic. A lot of people do. Since these are human traits, it's not unusual for you to identify with *all* of them, even though 1 or 2 will probably jump out at you. On the other hand, if you received a very low score on any style, something's up. Don't you have *any* traits of that particular style? If you don't, chances are, you're too attached to its opposite.

Yes, you may have noticed that these 6 styles represent the outer polarities of 3 traits:

- *Attention to Details:* The perfectionist pays too much attention to details; the dreamer doesn't pay enough attention.

- *Focus on the Future:* The worrier is too concerned about what might happen if; the crisis-maker is not sufficiently concerned (until crunch time).

- *Relating to Others:* The defier goes against what others want; the pleaser is excessively oriented to what others want.

Soon you'll be moving on to the chapters that provide a tailor-made change program for each style. Read these chapters in consecutive order or in the order of your ranked score. And please, don't skip over the last chapter, *"Making Change Happen."* But before you move on, I want you to appreciate a few key concepts that have driven my work.

Discover Your "But"

You can learn so much about yourself (and others) by paying close attention to where you place the word "But." Simply put, what you need to know is this:

Whatever comes *after the "But"* is what counts;

Whatever comes *before the "But"* simply softens the blow.

Intuitively, you already know this. If your boss says to you, "You're doing a good job but...," you brace yourself for the criticism. If your love says to you, "You're a great person but...," you prepare yourself for the rejection. Though you can't control what others say, you'll do yourself a great big favor if you place the *action-oriented part* of your message *after* the "But." If you don't, then this 3-letter word will be your never-ending excuse for why you fail to do what you're expected to do.

Oh, and one more thing. Know the difference between "But" & "And."

"But"

denotes opposition and blockage

"And"

denotes connection and resolution

Are you stuck on the BUT Excuse-way?	Or are you zipping ahead on the AND Speedway?
BUT I don't want to do it!	AND I'll get it done anyway!
BUT it's so difficult!	AND I'll ask for help.
BUT I love chatting on Facebook	AND I'll finish my work first.
BUT I want it to be perfect.	AND I'll complete it even if it's not perfect.

Next time you use the word "But" (which will probably be more frequent than you realize), add another clause that begins with the word "And" and notice that a solution is awaiting you!

When You Work the Program, the Program Works

You're almost ready to delve into the change programs. Each chapter provides you with strategies not only for taking action but also for enhancing your thinking and speaking skills. You may be surprised, however, to learn that there is no section for altering your feelings. Want to venture a guess why? After all, feelings control much of what we do or don't do.

Perhaps you figured it out. Feelings are highly resistant to conscious and deliberate modification. A friend tells you to be happy but you're feeling bummed out. Do you alter your emotional state just because she wants you to? Or even because *you* want to? Of course not. This doesn't mean that you have no control over your emotions; it simply means that the indirect approach works best.

Nathaniel Hawthorne explained it poetically.

*"Happiness is as a butterfly which, when pursued,
is always beyond our grasp, but which if you will
sit down quietly, may alight upon you."*

Charles Schulz, the creator of Peanuts, explained it more prosaically.

"Happiness is a warm puppy."

Get the idea? When you're doing what you like and being with people (or puppies) that you enjoy, happiness may alight upon you. But *force* yourself to be happy when you're not feeling it and it simply doesn't work. Happiness, accompanied by bona fide self-confidence, will be your luscious desert when you employ the strategies you'll learn in this book.

Does this mean that you're guaranteed to beat your procrastination habit once you finish this book? For some people, the answer is "yes." They put into practice what they learn. Others, however, have a huge disconnect between what they know and what they do. If you tend to be the latter, take on the challenge to make your learning more meaningful. Just like there's not a whole heap of difference between one who doesn't read and one who doesn't know *how* to read, it's also true that you may not notice much difference in how you operate *before* the program and *after* the program—*if* you don't use the tools you will be taught.

*"That which we persist in doing
becomes easier—not that the
nature of the task has changed, but
our ability to do it has increased."*
~ Ralph Waldo Emerson

So, let's begin right now to do some meaningful work. Take out a writing pad or open up a new document on your computer. I've got some questions for you to answer. This is a program, not simply a book. To get the most out of it, you need to put time and effort into it. None of the exercises I suggest are burdensome. No need to write a major essay. You won't be graded on your answers. On the other hand, don't be flippant. Reflect on the questions. The answers are not always obvious.

Getting to Know You

- What messages did your parents communicate to you—by words or deeds—about:

    spending time; wasting time?

    taking a risk; playing it safe?

    your strengths; your weaknesses?

  What impact did these messages have on you?

- As a child, what were your strengths? (You may not have thought of them as strengths; you probably just liked doing them or knew you were good at those types of tasks.)

- As a child, what were your weaknesses? (You may not have thought of them as weaknesses; you probably just hated doing them or had difficulty doing them.)

- Today, what strengths are you most proud of?

- Today, what weaknesses bother you the most?

- Do you see a connection between your weaknesses and your procrastination pattern? If so, elaborate on this.

That's it. You did it! Did you become aware of anything new from this first exercise? Not necessarily brand new. Just a different spin on the matter can often be incredibly useful in helping you to understand you.

> *"Make it your business to know*
> *yourself which is the most*
> *difficult lesson in the world."*
> ~ **Miguel de Cervantes**

THE PERFECTIONIST
PERSONALITY
...BUT I WANT IT TO BE PERFECT!

Welcome Perfectionists!

YOU HAVE MANY EXCEPTIONAL QUALITIES. You perform excellent work. You aspire to high standards. You're attentive to details. Yes, some may poke fun at perfectionists, calling them fusspots, nitpickers, or grinds. But others admire the sheer loftiness of their ambition. Shouldn't we *all* try to achieve the highest possible standards in whatever we do? Shouldn't we *all* strive for the best?

As you probably know, being a perfectionist is a more perplexing matter than simply striving for the best. The desire for perfection can sabotage your best efforts, frustrate you (and those around you) and breed procrastination. Despite your smarts, your over-the-top attention to details may be more of an impediment than an asset. In this chapter, you'll gain an in-depth understanding of your perfectionist personality—how it works for you and how it handicaps you.

But first, take a mini-version of the quiz you took earlier. See which of these questions resonate with you.

- Do I have a 'black or white' mentality, paying scant attention to the shades of gray between?

- Do I have difficulty completing a project because my own high standards haven't been met?

- Do I have difficulty maintaining a sense of humor while struggling to do a task I'm not good at?

- Do I get too preoccupied with details, rules or schedules that others don't seem to care much about?

- Am I reluctant to delegate tasks or get involved in a group project unless others do things *my* way?

If you answered *'yes'* to any of these questions, you've come to the right place. In your heart of hearts, you know that the way you deal with responsibilities is neither ideal nor pragmatic. Despite putting in considerable time and effort, you still tend to be displeased with yourself and your work. This is no way to live. You deserve better. It's time to create a future for yourself that doesn't drive you crazy and doesn't hold you back from being all you can be.

Let's begin by taking a look at two different perfectionist styles: the driven and the hidden.

Bob and Lori

Bob, a forty-eight-year-old self-employed accountant, is an open and avowed perfectionist. He freely admits that he's compulsive and only satisfied with himself when his work is flawless. His devotion to his goals is obvious to all who know him. He works long hours at the office, brings work home most nights and weekends, is married to his BlackBerry and typically looks pre-occupied and overburdened.

Since Bob is always working, it doesn't appear as though he's a procrastinator, but, in fact, he is. He seldom completes a project until there's an urgent deadline. Instead, he repeatedly finds one more thing to do to improve what he's working on. Though he admits that he imposes rigid demands on himself (and on those who work for him), he just can't settle for anything that he judges as "less than." Above all, he fears being criticized for not being "good enough." What a paradoxical scenario! Bob craves having a successful and pleasurable life, yet his work habits practically guarantee that his life will be far too pressured to enjoy.

Bob's procrastination at home creates a significant amount of family tension. He hasn't taken a real vacation in three years (despite his wife's pleading). He rarely gets around to helping his daughter with her school studies, even though "he'd like to." He's always "meaning" to read one of the biographies sitting on his bookshelf and he's always "going to" tackle one of the tasks on his list of home repairs that he admits needs to be done.

Bob's definitely more at ease with the detail-oriented world of work than with tending to family responsibilities. Even at work, however, there are times he feels disenchanted with his life, wondering why a 65+ hour work week is his norm, why he's so driven and why he rarely feels satisfied with his accomplishments.

Lori, a thirty-six-year-old journalist, presents as a fun-loving, easygoing personality who doesn't appear to have particularly high standards. To an outside observer, Lori projects a casual, even flippant attitude about assignments as she waits until the last minute to meet her deadlines. Though she wants to get the job done, she's easily seduced into attending to more appealing activities. At the last minute, she somehow manages to complete her writing assignment. However, her relief at completing it is tainted by the thoughts of how much better she could have done had she given herself sufficient time.

Lori's standards are so unrealistically high that she finds it difficult to forge ahead without becoming anxious. To protect her self-esteem, she "handicaps" the situation by starting late. This, in effect, creates a built-in excuse as to why she fails to meet her own intimidating standards. To protect her image, she doesn't let others see how much she cares. Indeed, even her best friend has no idea of the turmoil and discontent that lies beneath her carefully cultivated façade.

Last year, Lori received her dream assignment: a lead article for a major woman's magazine. One week before her article was due, a friend asked how it was going. The friend was flabbergasted when she blithely replied, "I'm just halfway through the first draft." After making up an excuse to her editor (poor grandma was at death's door one more time), Lori received an extended deadline. A month later, she did complete the assignment, managing to write an acceptable though unremarkable story. Her friend was once again startled when Lori remarked, "if only I'd had more time, I would have done a much better job." Privately, Lori berates herself for "dragging her feet," punishes herself for "screwing things up," and agonizes over what she "should have done." But will she change her pattern with her next assignment? Don't bet on it!

Different as they are from each other in personality and background, Bob and Lori are both perfectionist procrastinators. Despite their best intentions, they're not as happy or as fulfilled as they'd like to be. The good news: they're both motivated to change their patterns. Let's now look at the traits that all perfectionists have in common.

Thinking in Black or White

Perfectionists shy away from seriously considering any middle ground. Their choices: do a perfect job or don't do it at all. This attitude becomes increasingly problematic as perfectionists advance in their careers. Why? Because complex tasks rarely have perfectly definable outcomes. What's the perfect ad campaign? What's the perfect investigative report? There's certainly a difference between a poor one and an excellent one, but is there a perfect one? Striving for perfection makes sense with simplistic skills more geared toward elementary school, such as 100% on a spelling test.

Torn between the two alternatives of giving it all he's got or giving up, Bob usually opts for the former. This sounds good but seldom does life give him enough time, energy, or tranquility to do all that he needs to do to "be the best." By working too long and too hard on insignificant details, he postpones giving attention to other important areas of his life. Lori sabotages herself by initially choosing the second alternative—delaying the onset of work, guaranteeing herself the perfect excuse for why her work isn't as first-class as it could be.

Setting Unattainable Goals

Is it possible to have too high a goal? Absolutely! Going for what is unattainable is not a great strategy for achieving anything. Pushing yourself beyond your limits is not an effective way to go for the gold.

High achievers, in contrast to perfectionists, aim for excellence— not perfection. They define their objectives and evaluate their performance realistically, allowing themselves the freedom to establish flexible criteria for determining a successful outcome. Professional athletes, for example, set reasonable, season-by-season standards that are aimed at helping them realize their "personal best," not some superhuman vision of perfection. Similarly, they won't put off training on a given day because they suspect they might not perform as well as they should. Rather, they'll do their personal best in the context of each day that goes by. The mind-set of perfectionists, in contrast, is typically focused on doing their best, regardless of objective circumstances that need to be considered. The consequence: attainable goals get sacrificed in search of an elusive, impossible ideal.

Viewing Life as a Grind

Perfectionists tend to view many aspects of life as a burden, making it difficult for them to take tasks in stride. Whatever needs to be done becomes an ordeal as they focus on what's wrong, not on what's right; on what hasn't been done, not on what has been done. With expectations so high, perfectionists generally derive less satisfaction from day-to-day life than their non-perfectionist counterparts. Instead of being able to relax and have fun, they're forever focusing on their mistakes and mulling over what could and should be done to make things better. What's more, they continue to ruminate over past lapses and fret about future obligations. Like Bob, they wind up perpetually preoccupied—a poor state of mind for living well. Or, like Lori, they develop into chronic avoiders acting against time instead of working with time.

Not only is it tough for perfectionists to compliment themselves, it's also hard for them to accept compliments from others. What's more, perfectionists' need to be self-sufficient makes it hard for them to let others be of assistance. Thus Bob, the owner of his company, acts as more of a "doer" than a "manager" by refusing to delegate any of his huge workload. And Lori cuts herself off from helpful feedback from friends by pretending not to have a problem at all.

Fear of Failure, Fear of Success

Perfectionists are acutely aware that they may fail to live up to their own high standards. Not succeeding does not simply mean that the task wasn't performed up to par. It represents a personal indictment, triggering deep feelings of inadequacy, worthlessness and guilt. With such heavy emotions riding on success, it's no wonder they seek to avoid failure at all costs by dragging their heels on completing a project.

Compulsively doing more than they need to do is one method perfectionists use to keep failure at bay. Bob, for example, squanders precious time and energy attending to every detail of a project, continually adding praiseworthy touches to avoid intolerable imperfections. The upshot: tasks don't get done in a timely manner or are done with considerable angst accompanying each step of the project.

Perfectionists, like Lori, seek to sidestep failure by using pro-crastination as a defense. Their shaky logic goes as follows: If they choose not to take a particular challenge seriously—either by not doing anything about it or by treating it in an offhand, casual man-ner, they spare themselves the tyrannical, self-imposed need to be perfect. If they can create a situation in which circumstances are "beyond their control," they have the perfect excuse for not achieving perfection. Lori gives herself so little time to complete her assign-ments that she can't expect herself to do a perfect job—nor can anyone else who listens to her scoffing banter or observes her undisciplined behavior. Procrastination, she believes, is a better alternative than the unthinkable: using the full amount of available time and then not measuring up.

It's not just *the "fear of failure"* that can slow down a perfectionist's progress. It's also the *"fear of success."* Behind Bob's hesitancy to take on new professional opportunities is his fear that he might not live up to the increased demands that would be imposed upon him. As Irving Berlin said, *"The toughest thing about being a success is that you have to keep on being a success."*

For a perfectionist like Bob, success stirs up profound feelings of insecurity—feelings he expresses with the following questions:

> "Can I live up to the high expectations others will *now* have of me?"
>
> "Did I genuinely succeed or was I merely lucky?"
>
> "Why did reaching this level take me so long?"

Success raises the bar. New challenges, new hurdles, new problems—just thinking about these matters can send perfection-ists into a tailspin of anxiety. To gain a better understanding of how these characteristics get played out, let's now take a look at Lindsey's story.

Lindsey: A Perfectionist Personality

When I first met Lindsey, she described her major issue as a growing lack of confidence. Working as an investor relations manager, surrounded by movers and shakers, she felt an enormous pressure to succeed. Her idealized self-image made things worse. "I'm a legend in my own mind," Lindsey quipped, "always imagining I'll do things more spectacularly than others. Much to my chagrin, it rarely works out that way."

Lindsey's intense desire to achieve coupled with her meager self-confidence, gave rise to a number of complaints, expressed as:

> "I'd rather not do anything at all than do something just mediocre."

> "I have a hard time relaxing—even when I'm on vacation."

> "I get so worked up over little things that others don't care about."

As Lindsey continued to pour out her frustrations, it became obvious to me that perfectionism was an underlying factor in many of her issues. Though she felt compelled to meet the highest possible standards in whatever she attempted, she had neither the time nor energy to accomplish it all. The only way she discovered she could relieve some of the pressure was to put things off. Over the next few months, we explored how procrastination affected her work, her marriage, and her feelings of self-fulfillment.

One of the clearest signs of Lindsey's perfectionism was the distance between her ideal self-image and her actual self-image. Her ideal self, the self she claimed she "should" be, was that of a dazzling super achiever. Her actual self, however, fell far below that. Yes, she had an impressive career. But everybody in this company was exceptional and she wasn't sure she was keeping up with them. When she expressed this concern to a friend, her friend shot back, "Lindsey, cut yourself some slack; you're so hard on yourself!"

As our work progressed, Lindsey recognized how her perfectionism and low self-confidence were intermingled. For example, a troubling attribute was her difficulty applauding her own achievements. She once confessed: "When I receive a compliment, I don't take it in. I still have doubts, imagining that the person who gave me the compliment must have been too lazy to notice the mistakes I made. I'm convinced I got away with something. Not a great way to build up my ego, I know."

Lindsey's quagmire has a name. It's called the *"impostor syndrome"*—a common phenomenon among perfectionists. People with this syndrome believe that no matter how much they achieve, they're never really as competent, qualified or deserving as they appear to be. They're convinced that if someone were to scrutinize them closely enough, their cover would be blown. Lindsey was unable to shake the fear that some kind of disastrous "calling-to-account" would occur at the most unpredictable moment. In short: Lindsey felt like a phony.

Oh, if only Lindsey would take Cardinal Newman's philosophy to heart:

"A man would do nothing, if he waited until he could do it so well that no one at all would find fault with what he has done."

Ironically, though perfectionists try to control every aspect of what they do, they have difficulty believing that control of *their* success lies *within them.* Instead, they view the *locus of control* as lying somewhere outside their command: like in the hands of fate, a supervisor or even their subconscious. One way perfectionists seek to raise their success/failure ratio is to avoid taking on whatever might be too tough for them. By doing so, they limit their exposure to potential failure.

When she was younger, Lindsey used to think of herself as a "smart kid who could do anything." Now, however, that self-image felt pathetically weak compared to some of her peers who had achieved mega success. Perhaps she wasn't so clever. Perhaps she needed to take time off to figure out who she was and what she wanted out of life. In those quiet moments of solitude (which didn't happen very often), she found herself imagining a life that wasn't so driven, wasn't so pressured. Quite a change for a perfectionist!

> *"It's not the load that breaks you down, it's the way you carry it."*
> ~ **Lena Horne**

Procrastinating at Work

Initially, Lindsey derived a good deal of satisfaction from her job and from interacting with her colleagues. She loved working at full tilt, there was plenty of work to do and whatever she did, she did well. It took only a few mistakes and a few critical words for Lindsey's enthusiasm to fade. Any negative feedback she received was extremely painful. Hence, to prevent its re-occurrence, she decided it would be best if she would either work 100 percent on a project or let it go until she could. The result: over-preparing for every presentation, regardless of its level of importance to the business.

Other patterns plaguing Lindsey were so ingrained in her that she only began to understand them after months of coaching. For example, when she was near to completing a task, she would begin tearing it apart. She'd hunt for things that were wrong, then exaggerate their impact. Reviewing a subordinate's press release, Lindsey would gripe, "This press release is awful! We can't send it out." Thanks to her perfectionism, the need for a small edit would render the entire release unacceptable. Making matters worse, she'd misuse her own valuable time by rewriting the release from scratch.

Clearly, Lindsey had trouble setting reasonable time limits for her work projects. Instead of creating time-related milestones for the consecutive stages of a task, she took the attitude that everything remained "undone and re-doable" until the last conceivable moment. Taunted by her insecurities, Lindsey was forever finding reasons to revise her work, making it increasingly harder for her to meet deadlines. Referring to a long overdue report, she griped, "I get to a point where I feel that I've written a good report. But then I find one more thing that should be included. From then on, it's one delay after another." Understandably, she was stressed out. Though she complained of being *overworked,* she didn't recognize that *she was overworking.* Not a case of too much work in too little time; but too much time doing too much work.

Though Lindsey overworked some projects, with others she'd seek every excuse she could find, every diversion she could create, to drag her feet. Telling herself that she was gearing up to work on a project, she might spend an entire hour unnecessarily organizing and reorganizing papers. Finally, she might begin working for real, only to stop midstream and switch to something else. As a result of these habits, Lindsey had several unfinished projects on her desk and on her mind. To a superficial observer, it might have appeared that she was simply a bustling, busy worker. In fact, she was only behaving like a classic perfectionist procrastinator.

Procrastinating at Home

The need for perfection was creating havoc in Lindsey's home life. This was especially apparent in her approach to housekeeping. "I have high standards," she sighed. "It's a burden I wouldn't wish on my worst enemy. My home is my showcase and it reflects how people view me." If there were dirty dishes in the sink or dust on a table, Lindsey was simply unable to relax. She did indeed keep her home looking like a showcase.

Meanwhile, Lindsey's need for an unblemished household was creating tension in her marriage. She repeatedly fought with Scott over his messiness and unwillingness to do work that measured up to her standards. She interpreted his casual ways of doing household chores to mean that he must not care about her. Her reasoning: if he did care about her, he would accommodate her wishes. Scott, in turn, accused Lindsey of being a "control freak." These days he was doing even less around the house, so that it wouldn't appear as though he were caving in to her maddening over-the-top standards. By the time I met Lindsey, her marriage was at a breaking point.

When I asked Lindsey about her initial attraction to Scott, she responded. "I liked him right away because he was so easygoing. He was cute, funny, and I enjoyed the way he didn't take things so seriously." Yes, it's often true that as time goes on, a trait that was initially alluring to you is the same trait that gets under your skin. It wasn't long before Scott's easy-going nature turned from a desirable quality to a scorned one. Lindsey was forever criticizing her husband for what he had neglected to do. And even when Scott was in action mode, Lindsey was continually finding fault with the quality of his performance.

Lindsey's First Steps: Beginning the Change Program

Though it's hard for most people to shift their operating style, it's especially taxing for perfectionists. Why? Because shifting from a familiar pattern to an unfamiliar one creates temporary incompetence and discomfort. Not something perfectionists take in stride. Yet, Lindsey had had enough. She was determined to use her willpower to create a more satisfying life.

Lindsey began her change program by learning to *expand her options* instead of automatically assuming that there's only one "right" way to approach a problem. When faced with a new assignment, she generated several strategies for dealing with the task instead of insisting on only one. Her purpose in doing this was to train herself to think expansively instead of single-mindedly (some would say stubbornly). Over time, Lindsey reveled in the freedom and flexibility that this new approach provided. Now, it's your turn to discover how you can kick your procrastination habit by easing up on your perfectionism.

THE PERFECTIONIST'S CHANGE PROGRAM
Beat Your Procrastination Habit *and* Strive for Excellence

If you scored high on the perfectionist quiz, you probably noticed an abundance of similarities between Lindsey's way of living and your own. But you're not Lindsey. You've got your own history and style of living. Now it's time for you to pull the curtain aside and take a closer look at your story. Take a few moments to do a self-assessment exercise. Doing so will help you gain a deeper appreciation of your own issues. Be one of the 20% of readers who will *do* the exercise, not just skim through it. Remember, the program works if you work the program.

> *"Tell me I'll forget, show me, I may remember, but involve me and I'll understand."*
>
> **~ Chinese Proverb**

1. Recall an occasion when you spent an excessive amount of time and energy on a task, recognizing (after the fact) that you didn't need to do so much work. Reflecting on that occasion, answer these questions:

   • Why do you think you spent so much time on that project?

   • Looking back on it, was it worth it?

   • Could you have done as well if you spent *less* time on it? Why?

2. Recall a time when you wanted to complete a project on time but missed your deadline. For that occasion, ask yourself these questions:

   • What specifically kept you from finishing it in a timely way?

   • Were there any consequences for being late? Was your self-esteem tarnished? Were opportunities missed? Were relationships strained?

Congratulations! If you took the time to *do* the above exercise, you've shown that you're serious about understanding the dynamics of your procrastination. Armed with this understanding, you'll be in a better position to modify your patterns, making your desire for excellence pay off. Now, let's delve into specific strategies to help you beat your procrastination pattern. Experiment with these strategies, taking care not to become too compulsive about them. Remind yourself that change often happens slowly and in surprising ways. Be patient, sincere, and honest with yourself as you delve into the change program.

Guided Imagery for Your Creative Mind

Approach this guided imagery with a "let it be" attitude in which there are no right or wrong answers. Whatever image comes to your mind is fine. This exercise is designed to help you be more appreciative of your creative and spontaneous side.

Read the visualization slowly until you feel comfortable with its content. Then, either let someone else read you the instructions with a slow, relaxed voice or record these guidelines for your personal use which you can then replay whenever you wish. As you record the guided imagery, be sure to speak in a slow, soothing voice. Pause for thirty seconds between each instruction.

Assume a comfortable position in a place that's quiet, dimly lit, and free from distractions. Some people prefer lying down with their legs straight and slightly apart, their arms extended loosely at their side. Others prefer to sit in a relaxed mode in a comfortable chair, couch or bed.

Close your eyes and take a few deep breaths to clear your mind and relax your body—inhaling s-l-o-w-l-y through your nose, exhaling s-l-o-w-l-y through your mouth. Let go of any tension or tightness in your body. Allow the thoughts and cares of the day to drift away, leaving your body light, your mind empty.

In this relaxed state, picture a task that's been overwhelming you. *Let an image pop into your mind that represents this task.* Allow yourself to experience the negative emotions you feel when you're swamped with work. Slowly increase the muscular tension in your arms and legs as your anxiety level rises.

Now, picture this image slowly shrinking. As it shrinks, imagine it's not only getting smaller but attracting all the anxiety and negativity in your mind and body. The smaller the image becomes, the more relaxed you feel until you notice that *the image has turned into a small, black ball.*

Hold this ball in the palm of your hand. Now, imagine that the worrisome emotions you were feeling are no longer inside you but are contained within this ball which you're holding firmly in your grasp.

While still holding the ball, see yourself sitting comfortably under a tree in a beautiful meadow on a warm, spring day. Feel the soft grass beneath your body. Feel the warmth of the sun. Feel a gentle breeze in the air. See soft, white clouds floating across the sky.

Sitting under this tree, *imagine the small, black ball you're holding turning into a helium balloon.* You open your hand and release the balloon, watching it rise up, up, up into the sky and disappear from view. All you see is the blue sky and the white clouds going by.

Look back at your hand. *See a small red heart lying there.* Press this heart to your chest and feel it pass into your body easily and magically. Imagine the heart inside of you, slowly and rhythmically beating—filling you with a sense of peace and well-being.

Hear the nurturing voice of the heart telling you, *"I love you. I accept you just the way you are. If you take things easy, you will get them done. It doesn't have to be perfect; you don't have to be perfect."* As you embrace the warmth and acceptance of the message, feel your body at ease, your mind at peace.

Continue to relax, enjoying the moment. Notice how calm you feel when you're content with yourself. Take as much time as you need before you return to the present. With your eyes open and your body relaxed, *say something nurturing to yourself.* Believe it with all your heart.

Take time to absorb the meaning of your visualization before you move on to the next section.

Enhancing Your Thinking Skills

Admit that Perfectionism is Your Problem.

Nobody and I mean nobody is perfect. Not even you. Not even your idealized hero. You may have a perfect moment, perhaps even a perfect day. But you will not have a perfect life, a perfect relationship, a perfect career, no matter how hard you try. So, give up being a prisoner of your perfection. Don't insist that things be just right. And don't blame others when they're not.

Perfectionists tend to think of their problems as being "out there" somewhere. They wonder: "Why should I have to ease up on my standards? Others should do things the way they *should* be done." Let's face it; the world is not going to change to suit you. Yes, others could explain things better; they could be more efficient; they could be more careful, more considerate. They could, they could, they could. Yet, for the most part, they're not going to. We have limited control over others. If you repeatedly get fed up with situations—like your spouse's carelessness, your friend's lateness, or your supervisor's remoteness, speak up. But don't count on them changing. If they happen to change, that's a bonus. Acknowledge that your inability to chill out is a large part of the problem.

> *"Your assumptions are your windows on the world. Scrub them off every once in a while, or the light won't come in."*
>
> ~ **Isaac Asimov**

Give Yourself Sufficient Time to Accomplish Your Tasks.

Given your high standards, most undertakings will take you longer to do than you initially imagine. To make sure you have enough time to accomplish what you want to do, *take your most generous estimate, then add 20%.* For example, if you think you may need five hours to create a first draft of a report, budget six hours. If you're lucky and you don't need the extra hour, you've got it to enjoy any way you want. On the other hand, if you don't initially budget in the extra hour but wind up needing it, it's inevitable that you'll feel stressed.

In the same vein, when you're planning what you'd like to accomplish over a specified period of time (i.e. this week), avoid overloading your agenda. Instead, generate a down-to-earth list of probabilities (not possibilities), allowing a 20% margin of time for unanticipated glitches as well as enjoyable events you'd hate to pass up. Remember, life is not all about work.

Think More Realistically, Less Idealistically.

Perfectionists usually focus on the ideal way to perform a task. On occasion, this makes sense. With matters that are really important to you or vital to your goals, you may want to do an outstanding job. Yet, if you demand an outstanding job for everything you do—from work related projects to money management, from cooking to cleaning, you'll find yourself low on energy, high on irritability.

Instead of expecting or demanding the utmost from all your efforts, think of several possible ways to accomplish a task. Then narrow down the alternatives to the most pragmatic ones, given the time and resources you have available. In making this determination, don't forget to consider your past experiences handling similar tasks. Be aware of which strategies worked and which ones turned out to require Herculean effort.

To-Do Exercise

No time like the present to make a change. Start thinking more realistically right now. Choose a particular task you need to take care of. Be aware of how you're approaching it (or planning to, if you haven't started yet). Now evaluate your approach. Are you making the task bigger than it is? Is there a way you can do the task in a satisfactory manner, without making it an over-the-top achievement?

Here are a few things to consider. If you're expected to make a presentation at work, don't automatically start aiming to create a trailblazing talk on the topic. Instead, proceed calmly and rationally from the known facts:

- The nature of the team leader's expectations. Maybe she's only looking for a 10 minute summary of the work you've done while you're planning a major PowerPoint presentation that will be three times that length.

- Your genuine interest in the topic. If this is your pet project, go ahead and create an award-winning demonstration; if it's a "cover your ass" requirement, consider just doing the basics.

- The amount of time you can afford to devote to the project given the deadline date and your other responsibilities. No, you can't do it all. So, choose your priorities.

Now it's your turn. Write down ways that you can make a particular task easier, more enjoyable and possibly even more effective—without losing the essential quality of what you wish to achieve.

Aim for Excellence, not Perfection.

What's the difference between excellence and perfection? Dictionaries define perfection as "the condition of being flawless, the most desirable state imagined." Except perhaps in a simple multiple-choice test, perfection is difficult to envision, no less achieve. Contemplate, for instance, the perfect career, perfect life, perfect children, perfect spouse. Though you may have a general sense of what would be right for you, setting your sights on "perfect" is a breeding ground for disillusionment. (Ask anyone who thought they found their perfect soul mate.)

Dictionaries define excellence as "possessing superior merit, remarkably good." This is easier to envision, easier to achieve. Striving for excellence expands your mindset. Who knows where your talents and achievements will take you? Many highly successful people had no idea that they would be where they are now; they just worked hard and followed the opportunities. In contrast, striving for perfection keeps you measuring your work against some abstract standard that may be already outdated or meaningful only in your own mind.

As kids, many perfectionists were taught to "always do your best." This sounds like a good notion, but is often impractical. Given the limited time, energy, and resources of our busy lives, you simply can't do your absolute best in everything. So, think it through:

- If a certain task isn't important to you, you may just need to get it done in a run-of-the-mill manner to get it out of the way (i.e. tidy up, cook a meal).

- If a specific project represents something important to you, you'll want to put more effort into it (i.e. responding to a request, planning a party).

- If it's an undertaking in an area of life that's especially significant to you, then certainly "do your best." Even then, however, it's better to strive for excellence than outright perfection.

Be as Kind to Yourself as You Are to a Good Friend.

Make a conscious, consistent effort to be kinder to yourself. Sure it's helpful to recognize your errors and realize your shortcomings. But don't overdo it. Excessive self-criticism is not motivating; it's paralyzing. If you're tackling a task that's new, difficult, or outside your comfort zone, don't increase your discomfort with disparaging remarks. Disparagement nibbles away at your self-confidence. Hence, think more positive thoughts, such as:

- "It will be tough, but I can do it."

- "Once I get rolling on this, it'll get easier."

- "What the hell, I'll give it a shot."

If you're dissatisfied with a review or disappointed in your athletic exploits, tell yourself, "Setbacks happen to everyone. It doesn't mean I'm a failure." Experiencing setbacks, making mistakes, and even failing entirely to meet your objectives are all normal and typical. Indeed, they can be valuable ways of identifying your existing limits and, ultimately, learning to expand them.

> *"I have learned throughout my life as a composer chiefly through my mistakes and pursuits of false assumptions, not by my exposure to founts of wisdom and knowledge."*
>
> ~ Igor Stravinsky

Stravinsky's symphony *Rite of Spring* heralded in the 20th century. After that, he never stopped writing symphonies that are still considered a 'tour de force' in the music world. If Stravinsky can learn more from his mistakes than from the traditional pursuit of knowledge, so can you.

Enriching Your Speaking Skills

Change "Should" to "Could."

The word "should" connotes the *"right"* way to do something. And who decides what is the right way? It's an authority—could be your parent, your super-ego, your peer group, your mentor. Sure, some things you should do; I wouldn't want you thinking you shouldn't be brushing your teeth or stopping at stop signs. However, if you're a perfectionist, you've probably adopted a whole bunch of harsh and burdensome "shoulds." Eventually, you may come to believe that you have no choice in much of what you do. Instead of spurring you on to higher achievement, "shoulds" drain your energy. Hence, minimize the use of the word. Here's one way to do this:

Read these two sentences out loud.

"I *should* change my career."

"I *should* write a weekly blog."

Now replace "should" with "could".

"I *could* change my career."

"I *could* write a weekly blog."

What did you notice? Did you notice that "should" implies that there's only one "right" way to take care of what you want to do, when in fact, you have the freedom to choose when and how to do what you're contemplating. Did you notice that "could" is empowering, carrying the mature message that you have the right, capacity, and obligation to make a choice. Which career can I pursue? Do I have the time to write a weekly blog? After reflecting on potential options, you can then commit to the one that you think is best, without guilt and doubt plaguing you.

To-Do Exercise

Now it's your turn. Write down a sentence relating to your personal or work life that begins with *"I should."* Keep the same sentence but change "should" to "could." Reread the sentence.

What difference did it make when you changed one little word? Was the "could" sentence more inspiring to you? Did the "should" sentence seem more burdensome? If not, try it one more time with another sentence. Again, I'm not suggesting that the word "should" be eliminated from your vocabulary. I am suggesting, however, that you use it less frequently.

Change "I have to" to "I want to."

Listen to the words you choose. Notice how often you use the phrase "have to," as in: "I have to meet my friend tonight" or "I have to practice my speech now." "Have to" implies coercion. It suggests that you're undertaking an action only because you're being made to. This makes your work feel more onerous than it needs to be. Give yourself an incentive to act rather than forcing yourself to act. Own up to your responsibilities by saying that you "want to," not that you "have to."

"I want to meet my friend tonight" is, of course, easy for you to admit. Saying, "I want to practice my presentation now," may seem like pure bull. But that's only if you're reflecting on the short-term, not the long-term. Sure you can think of better ways to spend your time than to review your presentation. But let's face it. You're making that presentation for a reason. Maybe it's for a cause dear to your heart or for a career advancement seminar. Hence, even if you can't work up the enthusiasm for wanting to practice your presentation, you can certainly acknowledge that you want it to be good because you know what it might mean for your reputation, your company or your long-term goals.

Minimize Your Use of Evaluative Language.

Perfectionists typically use turbo-charged language when evaluating an event. To temper your tendency toward doing this, use more descriptive words, less evaluative words. Rather than describing an admired figure as "unimpeachably brilliant," use more descriptive words, like, "I find him to be informative and enlightening."

Don't forget, too, to moderate your words when you're upset with yourself. Hear the difference between:

"I screwed up that interview. I'm such an idiot.
What's wrong with me?"

and

"I didn't handle that interview well. I need to improve
my interview skills;
I sure don't want that to happen again."

Be a good friend to yourself. No need for you to be your toughest critic. Plenty of others are perfectly willing to do that job for you.

To-Do Exercise

Think of some aspect of your life in which you're displeased with yourself. Now pretend you are your harshest critic. (I know, you may not have to pretend.) Write down a few phrases in which you berate yourself for not doing enough or not being enough.

Now imagine that you are your dearest friend. Write down a few phrases in which you are kind to yourself, accepting yourself the way you are—even if you don't particularly admire some of your traits.

Notice how you feel when you speak to yourself kindly rather than harshly. Do you think you have the ability to achieve more when you treat yourself well or when you crack the whip without mercy? Why?

Expanding Your Acting Skills

Make a To-Do List that's Short and Practical.

It's a good idea to have a to-do list. If you're a perfectionist, however, it's likely that your list is too long, too detailed, and too intricate. If you put *everything* on your list, you'll practically guarantee being disappointed with what you've accomplished, though in actuality, you may have accomplished a great deal. To prevent this from happening, revise your list. Make it short and practical. Guard against including every possible task you'd like to get done. Concentrate, instead, on what's highest priority for you. Resist the impulse to fill up every hour. Give yourself unscheduled time to cope with the unexpected or simply to relax—without any agenda.

If your list is written on paper, use a pen and then cross off items after you've completed them. Don't be like a client of mine who wrote her list in pencil, erasing each item as she completed it. What's the problem with that? No visible record of accomplishment. No recognition of all the work she did. Hence, no pat on the back even though it was well deserved. If your to-do list is digital, the same situation can happen. Don't delete each item on your list as soon as you've taken care of it. Rather, put a star next to it to indicate that you've completed it; a double star for a tough task particularly well done. If you think it's only kindergarten kids who appreciate a gold star, you're wrong. We all do.

Assign a Time Limit for Completing Each Task.

Time is finite. We each have twenty-four hours in a day to get things done and a hefty number of those hours are spent sleeping, grooming, eating and doing maintenance activities (like laundry or cleaning up after yourself). Include social activities and dealing with the unexpected and you'll find there's only a limited amount of time left over for other activities.

To guarantee that you appropriate a reasonable amount of time for the work you've been putting off, write out a "time budget" for tasks on your to-do list. For example:

Review Report: 1 hour

Respond to Emails: 30 minutes

Cook Dinner: 40 minutes

If you're a member of the Facebook generation, you already know that social networking, web surfing, or blogging can take up an inordinate amount of time. So add those to your time budget as well:

Social Networking: 40 minutes

Gaming: 30 minutes

Responding to blogs: 20 minutes

Make sure your time budget doesn't have more hours accounted for than there are hours in the day. In determining time frames, reflect on your past experiences with similar activities. Then allow yourself 20% percent more time to handle unexpected developments. If you're not keeping up with your time budget, tweak it, don't drop it.

Let Technology or Other People Help You Set Time Limits.

You may not be the best judge of how long tasks take. Perfectionists are notorious for either underestimating the time (they forget how much attention they pay to details) or overestimating the time (imagining everything is a big deal). Hence, you may want to consult with a colleague, supervisor or spouse to see how long they think a task will take.

In some cases, the task may be one that you've never previously undertaken—such as learning a new computer program. If so, the most likely resource for estimating the time may come from someone who has previously done the work. In other cases, such as estimating how much time you'll spend online, decide beforehand what you'll do. Because it's so easy to get sucked into spending more time than you planned, use technology—a beeper, a buzzer, a computer pop-up to remind you that your time is up. Without such a reminder, it's likely that you'll spend an excessive amount of time on one activity to the detriment of your other obligations.

Don't Do More than Your Fair Share of Work with Group Projects.

You may occasionally find yourself working with others on a work, organizational, or home project. In such group activities, you may be inclined to take on more than your fair share of tasks. Don't! Since you like things done the way they "should" be done, you may find yourself doing the bulk of the work yourself or redoing what someone else did. Initially, this may seem like no big deal. However, too often the upshot is:

- Resentment *toward* others, displeasure *from* others

- Lack of time available for your other projects

- Feeling over-burdened with responsibilities

Puncture the fantasy that you can or should take over a group project—even if indeed, your way is better.

Make One Deliberate Mistake Each Day.

There's no better way to change your "it's gotta be perfect" tendencies than to practice being imperfect. Make a mistake. Make it deliberately. By doing so, you may learn to cope with blunders and shortcomings in a more gracious manner. What's more, you may discover what truly needs your precious attention and what you can overlook, without any significant consequences.

For example, if you're in the habit of keeping your desk excessively neat, try deliberately leaving it messy for a whole week. If you make your bed every morning, don't do it for three days in a row. If you're always early for appointments, come five minutes late to the next one. Sure you'll be uncomfortable doing these things, but so what? Hopefully you'll discover that on occasion doing things in a less than perfect manner is not such a big deal. After all, you want some spontaneity in your life, don't you?

> *"Anyone who has never made a mistake has never tried anything new."*
> ~ **Albert Einstein**

Don't Just "Do"; Let Yourself "Be."

A fulfilling life is not only about doing; it's also about being, enjoying, luxuriating in _____ (you fill in the blank). If you're like many perfectionists, you may think that if you're not working on some chore, you're wasting time. Hence, as soon as you finish one undertaking, you're on to the next.

Counteract the tendency to define yourself solely in terms of what you do. Create downtime to relax, revitalize your energy and do absolutely nothing. Regularly allow yourself time "to be." If you don't know what it's like to just "be," ask any adolescent. They are experts at it. And review this list:

- Hanging with friends or family (with no particular agenda)

- Taking a casual stroll or bike ride

- Browsing in an interesting store

- Listening to music

- Taking a nap

- Relaxing in the sun

Now add at least five more ideas to this list. Come on, do it! The harder it is for you to do, the more you need to do it. You don't want to be one of those people who never find time to enjoy themselves, do you?

Ending Exercise

Congratulations Perfectionists! You've completed this chapter. Now take a moment to simply relax and breathe easily. There's so much valuable information in each chapter. Although you can read it all you can't absorb it all—not right away. So, review the change program and choose 1, 2, or 3 skills that you will implement this week. Once you've gotten those under your belt, then go back for more. This program is designed to be *a reference* for you. Take in what you can use now. When you're ready to incorporate more skills, return to the program and see what's next for you.

Ease Up on Yourself
then
Celebrate your Amazing Achievements!

CHAPTER 4

THE DREAMER PERSONALITY
...BUT I HATE DEALING WITH THOSE ANNOYING DETAILS!

Welcome Dreamers!

YOU HAVE MANY OUTSTANDING QUALITIES. You're creative. You're imaginative. You may even be a visionary. So what could be holding you back? Here's the rub. Too often you become enamored with an idea, but don't follow through with doing what must be done to make it happen. Without dedicated work, your creative ideas end up nowhere—while you end up disappointed in yourself and quite possibly in life itself.

No matter how smart you are, work still needs to be done. Even Albert Einstein did not rely solely on his super power brain. He attributed his success to his work habits, saying;

"It's not that I'm so smart, it's just that I stay with problems longer."

In this session, you'll gain a better understanding of your dreamer personality—how it helps you and how it handicaps you. But first, take a mini-version of the quiz you took earlier. See which of these questions resonate with you.

- Do I think a lot about what I'd like to accomplish but rarely get projects off the ground?

- Do I wait for opportunities to drop into my lap rather than take an active "go get 'em" approach?

- Do I let time drift by with passive activities like daydreaming, watching TV or casually surfing the Web?

- Do I spend more time thinking about the finished project than thinking about the details needed to get it done?

- Do I long to be able to go from A to Z without dealing with all those bothersome details in between?

Eleanor Roosevelt stated that, *"The future belongs to those who believe in the beauty of their dreams."* Yet the future is anything but beautiful for those who spend a multitude of their time dreaming, minimal time doing. The capacity to develop innovative ideas and inspiring designs is one of your greatest assets. But those dreams can end up being nothing more than fantasies if you live *in* your dreams instead of living *out* your dreams. Neglecting to put in sustained effort can mean that the future you dream about will be very slow in arriving, if it arrives at all.

Though dreamers may embrace supersized notions, it's not unusual for them to wonder why they aren't receiving rave reviews. "I have so many great ideas" said one of my favorite dreamers, "but somehow my ideas never see the light of day." It took awhile for this gifted man to appreciate the bottom line: No action, no achievement—despite a whole lot of creativity. This is no way for a visionary to live. You deserve better. It's time for you to create a future that will come true.

Let's now take a look at two different types of dreamer personalities: Jason, the vague laid-back style and Andrea, the dependent, narcissistic style.

Jason and Andrea

Jason, a would-be professional musician, illustrates one variant of the dreamer procrastinator that I call the laidback style. He has trouble committing himself to a career, opting instead to keep on entertaining whatever possibilities interest him in the moment. The upshot: he doesn't hone in on any possibility long enough for even one of them to serve as a viable starting point for serious achievement. When asked about his future, he quips, "I want to be rich and famous. And make a difference. I know I have talent. But nothing seems to be happening. Maybe I'll win the lottery and get rich that way." By his own admission, Jason feels embarrassed that he doesn't know how to move ahead career-wise. Such is the legacy of years spent daydreaming rather than performing work in a thoughtful, attentive and sustained manner. His pattern is to hope for good fortune rather than to work out a viable to-do plan.

Jason's free-spirited lifestyle includes occasional musical gigs, bit acting jobs, working out, hanging out, helping friends out. Over the past ten years, he's taken on temporary work that has allowed him to get by financially (along with help from his parents). Publicly, he claims that he doesn't want to "sell out" by getting a steady job or pursuing dull office work. Privately, he acknowledges how insecure he is about what to do with his life.

At first, people perceive Jason as a creative and charismatic guy. Over time, however, they see him as more scatterbrained than creative. When close friends encourage him to be more grounded about work, he's quick to segue into another topic. Jason's worried girlfriend has also tried to motivate him to take specific career action. Though he admits to being easily distracted, he discounts her concerns—claiming that she's just a nervous personality by nature. Employing his self justifying, dreamy logic, he rationalizes her critique by claiming that his procrastination is a bigger problem for her than it is for him.

Andrea, a social worker who works with an immigrant population, is another variant of the dreamer personality that I call the dependent type. Initially, she presents as a heroic-scale doer on a mission to save the world. Time after time, she rescues clients from near disaster as she decries the injustices of life to all who will listen to her. Inevitably, it becomes clear that though Andrea highlights the big rescue projects, it's always tomorrow when she needs to take care of routine day-by-day tasks. Her lack of attention to detail (i.e. a form not filed in a timely way) too often *creates* the crisis that requires her to come to the rescue of her clients.

Just as she relies on others to handle mundane office details, Andrea counts on her husband to take care of the practical side of their life together. From money matters to organizational matters, she remains dreamily out of touch. She doesn't interpret this type of dreamer dependency as unfair: Why shouldn't others do for her, since she does "everything" for others? Why, she wonders, is she, "the good one," unappreciated, unrewarded and misunderstood?

Despite their differences, both Jason and Andrea exhibit the following typical dreamer traits:

Taking a Passive Approach to Life

Since dreamers live so much in their heads, they tend to be passive rather than active in taking care of their obligations. Instead of being responsible about money, they count on winning the lottery, attracting a wealthy patron, or inheriting money from a surprise source. Rather than acknowledge the relative mediocrity of their work and the corresponding need to put more time and effort into it, they sink back into visions of "someday" and "somehow" they'll astound all with the unprecedented brilliance of their accomplishments.

As they indulge in this kind of 'wait and see' fantasizing, dreamers put off acquiring the self-discipline and life management skills that would ultimately serve them well. Jason, for example, flips back and forth between spells of disappointment over his lack of career success and ecstasies of relief based on pot-induced reveries. Rather than take steps to find the happy middle ground of a well planned, well executed, and well enjoyed lifestyle, he sinks into the purer form of mental procrastination formally known as omphaloskepsis—"the contemplation of one's navel."

Though Andrea presents herself as a grand rescuer, her day-to-day existence feels unfulfilling and unexciting. It's as if she were waiting for something or someone to rouse her to action. Though she views herself as a "savior of the poor," her own life is poorly managed and she doesn't have a clue why.

Giving Insufficient Attention to Facts and Details

Dreamers spend more time thinking and talking about a project than actually *doing* anything about it. They prefer being swept up in generalities rather than tying themselves down to a particular way of doing things. As a result, they don't pay enough attention to the 'who, what, where, when, why and how' details that are necessary to bring a task to fruition. Though they may be as smart as any of their peers, ignoring the how-to part of a project eventually creates a true lack of competence.

Dreamers often act as though particular abilities are beyond them. Psychologist Dr. Martin Seligman calls this pattern *"learned helplessness."* Once you believe you cannot do a task, you act as though it's true. In reality, these are skills that dreamers may not want to do, may not enjoy doing, haven't tried to do or haven't given enough effort to learn them well. Such skills will continue to haunt them, until they learn to actively approach the task rather than passively avoid it.

Convinced that they're helpless to perform certain projects or procedures, dreamers rely on others to do their work or worrying. Jason, for instance, states that his own procrastination is a bigger problem for his girlfriend than for himself. Instead of getting around to doing what he needs to do to advance his musical career (or any other career), he spends his time spinning out task-avoiding thoughts and fantasies. And Andrea resorts to dependent helplessness to get others to take on the tasks that she believes are beyond her or beneath her. Unfortunately, neither Jason nor Andrea abides by Eleanor Roosevelt's wisdom when she asserted that in life,

"You must do what you think you cannot do."

Avoiding Distressful Work

Dreamers long for life to be easy and enjoyable. With this goal as their guide, they coast through life in a dreamy state of disengagement. Imagining the ideal life as one that's free from setbacks and defeats, they seek magical solutions to propel them to success. Their focus on feeling good in the moment makes them lose sight of what might, in fact, make them feel good on a long-term basis. Instead of aiming for deeper satisfaction by taking on tough tasks and thought-provoking challenges, they indulge in insubstantial reveries as their dreams recede even further from possibility.

We see this trait most obviously in Jason's life. Rather than seeking pride in mastering new proficiencies, he resorts to immediate, short-lived gratification that he's always relied upon: hanging with friends, getting high, doing what he feels like in the moment. These activities keep him from recognizing how he's compromising his future by over-indulging his present. This comfort orientation manifests itself more subtly in Andrea's life. Strangely enough, she's more comfortable with the role of "grand rescuer," less comfortable with taking care of the daily grind details of life. Taking care of non-heroic chores and responsibilities is just not her thing.

Putting in Less Hours

Some dreamers believe that they're ahead of their time. If only others would 'get' their visions, they'd be sitting pretty with fame and fortune. Though others may indeed be impressed with their visions, work still needs to be done. And that is the dreamer's weak spot. How does the dreamer deal with the work? Often by:

- *Seducing* family members into doing their chores

- *Persuading* friends to take care of their personal business

- *Conning* colleagues and supervisors into giving them second chances

- *Letting* it go until they get into serious trouble

When dreamers develop an inappropriate dependence on others to do the grunt work, they simply don't gain the knowledge and skills required to function well on their own. What starts out as a clever maneuver to get what they want becomes an unhealthy dependency. This dependency may be experienced as weakness ("I hate asking others for help") or as false entitlement ("I'm special; I shouldn't have to do the nuts and bolts work"). Not the best strategy for success. Not the best strategy for getting along in the world.

Hence, Jason would rather wait for good fortune to strike than to put in the needed effort to create his own fortune. Since he's convinced himself that he's special, it's a natural next step to believe that good fortune will ensue. Because Andrea's social work is so important, she has come to believe that other aspects of life are not worth her time. Why waste time and energy dealing with distressing details? It would be breaking the faith.

To gain a better understanding of how these characteristics get played out in the life of a dreamer personality, let's now take a look at Brett's story.

Brett: A Dreamer Personality

Nothing portrays success more than professional presentation. At least that's what Brett believes. He dresses well, speaks well, and presents as a creative and charismatic charmer. He introduces himself to new business prospects as a serial entrepreneur. He believes he is quickly going to rise to the top—with new notions about pet products, green technology and health services for the boomer population. It all sounds great. His enthusiasm is contagious; his creativity is catching. Too bad, his procrastination patterns prevent him from even approaching the finish line.

Distractions, digital and non-digital, have always been Brett's nemesis. A book beckons, a soul mate summons, Angry Birds chirp, Twitter tweets, e-mail dings. A never-ending source of distractions impinges on his day. And that doesn't count the invited interruptions: the social calls he encourages, the errands he runs, the articles he reads. The novelty of the new beats the tedium of the old every time.

Procrastinating at Work

When Brett arrived at his first coaching session, I asked him to tell me about his work history. Turns out he wasn't always working for himself. Just a few years ago he was the "idea man" at a prestigious industrial design firm. His employer was impressed with projects he proposed, in particular, a chair capable of giving each user a customized massage based upon their physical needs. After a period of time, the deadline for the next step of the project arrived. The firm's partners gathered in the conference room to review the progress he had made in developing plans for the showcase massage chair that they were going to unveil at a major trade show. But the prototype was far from ready. In fact, their acclaimed "idea man" had not advanced much beyond the last meeting in which he had pitched his idea.

Yes, he'd researched competitive projects, but had yet to analyze their specs. He'd not gotten around to conducting the focus groups he had said he would. He hadn't even arrived at a cost analysis of the product, offering only a ballpark estimate based on his "intuitive inkling" of what something like this should cost. The partners watched in disappointment and disbelief as Brett simply reiterated his initial concept. After the presentation, the partners made two quick decisions: There would be no mention at the trade show of any wondrous new massage chair. And their resident genius was fired.

Did this faze Brett? Only briefly. He decided he was destined for better things anyway. He would do it on his own. He would work from home—a dream come true. No more sucking up to demanding bosses, office politics or snooze-inducing meetings. Wake up when you want, dress in sweats, hit the gym mid-day. How did this new work environment work out for Brett? You guessed it. Things went from bad to worse. Though working on your own can be a dream come true for a well-organized person, for a dreamer like Brett, it spelled disaster.

My initial impression of Brett was of a charming, upbeat man who appeared to be a go-getter temporarily down on his luck. But as he continued to speak, I began to wonder how grounded he was. His speech was full of hyperboles—all the things he intended to do were "huge," "important," and "unprecedented." And yet, his grandiose plans weren't supported by any move-ahead efforts. Where was the substance behind the notions? Too many discrepancies existed between his imagined self and his real-life experiences.

Though Brett had been "let go" from several positions for the same reason that he had been fired from the design firm (a failure to follow up words with deeds), he blamed his failures on the poor economy and the preposterous expectations of others. During his most honest moments of introspection, however, he knew that something was amiss with the way he functioned. He simply didn't feel "real." And that triggered deep feelings of shame and embarrassment. The only piece of good news that was coming his way: he finally had a name for what had been haunting him—he was a classic dreamer procrastinator.

The sheer number of jobs Brett had held in his young life testified to his dreamer tendency. Though he was initially energized by the all-things-possible aspect of new ventures, he quickly tired of the ventures when detailed work was demanded of him. Viewing himself as an exceptionally creative person, Brett belittled many of his job-related tasks, considering them too simplistic or mundane for any prolonged attention. The upshot: Either these tasks didn't get done or they were done poorly with a last minute rush job approach.

Procrastinating at Home

Brett's dreamer procrastination style was not limited to his work environment. When Brett landed his "break-through" job at the design firm, he'd spent major money on an executive wardrobe and luxury set of wheels. Though he didn't have the cash to pay for these purchases, he rarely let such facts pin him down. He had to have the expensive accoutrements to provide tangible support for his private notion that he was a rising star. When the bills began pouring in, he put them in a drawer: out of sight, out of mind. He convinced himself that he didn't need to deal with them now. He could leverage himself, since his future success was all but guaranteed. Unfortunately, the creditors didn't see it that way, nor did his wife, who was anxious and distressed about his spending habits. Though Brett agreed to cut down on his spending, he did so only for a limited period of time. "Have faith," he told his wife. "One day, we'll have no more money problems, I promise." Regrettably, Brett was oblivious to the fact that "one day" is no specific day at all.

As for household management tasks, Brett handled them much the way he handled tasks at work. Because his grandiose self-image created a heightened sense of entitlement, his prevailing attitude toward housework was relaxed, at best. Though he felt loving toward his wife, who worked full-time, he subtly made it known that per-forming routine chores and repairs wasn't his thing. He'd put them off to watch a game or practice his golf swing, saying that there'd be plenty of time to take care of "drudge work." Yet, that time was always slow in arriving.

Paradoxically, when Brett did take on a creative household challenge, he'd inflate it into such a monstrous project that he was almost certain never to complete it. He'd begin with a big wave of enthusiasm, throwing himself into the task with gusto. Before long, however, the wave would wither away. His incentive to work would dissolve. His enthusiasm would fade into a lazy stupor.

A recent example: Brett was enthusiastic about refinishing an antique chest of drawers. After contemplating the job, purchasing brushes and paint, he decided that the whole bedroom would need to be repainted and several pieces of furniture would need to be replaced to do justice to the project. The ever enlarging task soon became so overwhelming that it was abandoned. The antique chest with its worn-off finish still languishes in the attic, six months later.

Presently, Brett feels trapped in a three pronged dilemma: He doesn't like structure being imposed upon him; he doesn't impose structure on himself; he craves more structure in his life! What's a dreamer to do? "I see now that others have a clearer sense of what they want and how to get it," Brett lamented. "What I want is hazy; hence I don't make good use of my time. I can easily fritter away the whole day, consoling myself about it, by saying, 'I'm entitled to have a lazy day.' But to be perfectly honest, I know I have plenty of lazy days. It would be great to get a better grip on my time."

Despite moments of despair, Brett knew that he had strengths that could serve him well. He was intelligent, creative, easygoing, and enjoyed people. Quite a list of assets! It therefore pained him to see so many of his friends moving ahead on the road to success while he was still floundering. Often, he'd feel consumed with envy. "Why not me?" he wondered. In his more reflective moments, Brett knew the answer. Others went after what they wanted and continued to work at it until they achieved success. He had spurts of activity, but was weak with follow-through. Knowing that, however, did not prove to be a sufficient motivator—until now.

Brett was ready to appreciate Julie Andrews' take on discipline:

"Some people regard discipline as a chore.
For me, it's a kind of order that sets me free to fly."

Brett's First Steps: Beginning the Change Program

Brett was so oriented toward the state of "feeling good in the moment" that I believed it would help if we began with augmenting his ability to be self-disciplined. I advised Brett to notice each time he impulsively decided to do something to "feel good." When that happens, I said, ask yourself: "Will this make me feel good *about myself* or will I just feel good for the moment?"

At our next appointment, Brett was delighted with how effective this shift in thinking was. "Right away, I noticed how often I spend my time on whatever pleases me in the moment. When I flipped on the TV to watch a game, I asked myself *the* question. I knew immediately that watching the game would not make me feel better about myself. So, I picked my butt up off the couch and got right into taking care of a long neglected task at home. Though I didn't like doing it, after it was done, I did have a sense of accomplishment."

As we continued our work together, Brett adopted additional easy-to-learn techniques to decrease his inclination toward dreaming at the expense of doing. Now, it's your turn to discover how you can make your dreams come true.

THE DREAMER'S CHANGE PROGRAM
Beat Your Procrastination Habit *and* Nurture Your Dreams

If you scored high on the dreamer quiz, you probably noticed an abundance of similarities between Brett's way of living and your own. But you're not Brett. You've got your own history and style of living. Now it's time for you to pull the curtain aside and take a closer look at your story. Take a few moments to do a self-assessment exercise. Doing so will help you can gain a deeper appreciation of your own issues. Be one of the 20% of readers who will *do* the exercise, not just skim past it. Remember, the program works if you work the program.

> "Tell me I'll forget, show me,
> I may remember, but involve
> me and I'll understand."
> **~ Chinese Proverb**

1. Recall an occasion when you had a task to do but somehow never got around to doing it. For that occasion, ask yourself these questions:

    • What specifically was your stumbling block toward doing the work?

    • What negative consequences did you experience because you didn't do the job?

2. Recall a time when you completed your work but got it done after the deadline. For that occasion, ask yourself these questions:

    • What specifically kept you from working efficiently?

    • Were there any consequences for being late? Was your self-esteem tarnished? Were opportunities missed? Were relationships strained?

Congratulations! If you took the time to *do* the above exercise, you've shown that you're serious about understanding the dynamics of your procrastination. Armed with this understanding, you'll be in a better position to modify your patterns and make your creativity pay off. Now let's delve into specific strategies to help you beat your procrastination pattern.

Guided Imagery for Your Creative Mind

It may seem counterproductive for a dreamer to spend more time with imagery, as it's likely you already spend too much time living in your head. However, this exercise is designed to specifically help you turn those amorphous dreams into attainable achievements.

To begin, read the visualization slowly until you feel comfortable with its content. Then, either let someone else read you the instructions with a slow, relaxed voice or record these guidelines for your personal use which you can then replay whenever you wish. As you record the guided imagery, be sure to speak in a slow, soothing voice. Pause for thirty seconds between each instruction.

Assume a comfortable position in a place that's quiet, dimly lit, and free from distractions. Some people prefer lying down with their legs straight and slightly apart, their arms extended loosely at their side. Others prefer to sit in a relaxed mode in a comfortable chair, couch or bed.

Close your eyes and take a few deep breaths to clear your mind and relax your body—inhaling s-l-o-w-l-y through your nose, then exhaling s-l-o-w-l-y through your mouth. Let go of any tension or tightness in your body. Allow the thoughts and cares of the day to drift away, leaving your body light, your mind empty.

In this relaxed state, picture yourself standing in a park *holding the strings to three helium balloons: one red, one yellow, and one green.* You look up and admire the three balloons, swaying in the blueness of the sunny sky. As you look closely at each balloon, you see a dark, vague shape inside each one—though you can't quite make out what any of these shapes are.

Picture the balloons bumping into each other. Feel them tugging on the strings you're holding. See these motions increasing in intensity until it becomes uncomfortable to keep on holding the strings. As you look around, you *notice a waist-high pole in the ground near you.* The pole has a hook on the end of it that you tie all three balloons to.

You grab hold of the string to the red balloon, pull it down to the ground and burst it open with a pin. There, among the fragments, you see a flat wooden square. You realize it is the floor piece to a miniature house. You place it on the ground to the right of you.

Now, grab hold of the string to the yellow balloon, pull it down to the ground and burst it open with a pin. There, among the fragments, you see four small wooden squares. You realize these four pieces are the walls to the house. You turn to your right and fit each wall piece into a groove on the floor piece until the walls are in place.

Finally, you grab hold of the string to the green balloon, pull it down to the ground and burst it with a pin. There, among the fragments, you see a small wooden roof. Taking it into your hand, you turn to your right and place it on top of the four walls of the house.

Now, step back and admire the miniature house that you've built. Watch it slowly expand until it becomes an attractive full-size house. You enter the house and notice a cozy chair by a roaring fireplace. You sink into this chair and relax. When you're completely at ease, you hear a voice within saying, *"You've done a good job. When you take matters into your own hands and work diligently on them, you can build great things."*

Continue to relax, taking comfort in the words you've just heard. Notice the satisfaction you feel when you've done what you set out to do. Take as much time as you need. Whenever you're ready, slowly open your eyes. With your eyes fully open, say something inspiring about your ability to make things happen. Believe it with all of your heart. Absorb the meaning of your visualization before you move on to the next section.

Enhancing Your Thinking Skills

Appreciate the Difference between Daydreams and Goals.

Daydreams are visually appealing images: a status home, a professional award, a best-selling novel. A goal, in contrast, involves a plan with an explicit structure. It's best when a goal has:

- Objectives that you clearly define

- Steps you'll take to achieve those objectives

- Time frames for meeting each step

- Resources you'll utilize

- A goal line to know when you've achieved your objective

Continue to enjoy your dreams. But, whatever you're truly striving for, make it a goal. Then, map out the road you'll take to reach that goal.

> *The key factor separating geniuses from the merely accomplished is not a divine spark. It's not I.Q., a generally bad predictor of success. Instead, it's deliberate practice. Top performers spend more hours (many more hours) rigorously practicing their craft.*
>
> **~ David Brooks**

Appreciate the Difference between Feeling Good and Feeling Good About Yourself.

Feeling good about yourself, as opposed to simply feeling good, has to do with taking pride in your accomplishments. On a short-term basis, you may not feel good as you push yourself to go to the gym or work on a complex project. On a long-term basis, however, the self-confidence and self-respect you'll gain from completing these activities will make you feel enduringly good about being yourself.

Guard against your proclivity to seek pleasure from being passive—just letting time and deadlines drift on by as you watch TV, surf the Web or lounge in the sun like a lizard on a rock. Certainly being passive on occasion is fine, but if you stay in that state too often or for too long, it's likely to be at the expense of your self-esteem and well-being.

Guard Against Thinking of Yourself as 'Special.'

There are countless ways that you can go about creating troublesome, ultimately self-deluding gaps between your private image of yourself and your public image. Hence, it's a good idea to stay on top of your thoughts by asking yourself questions like, "Am I inflating my accomplishments?" or "Am I getting carried away here?"

You may catch yourself modifying a past experience so that in your narrative, your actions come off more favorably than what actually occurred. You may recreate a time when you failed an exam as a time when you refused to take the exam seriously on principle, leaving the reluctant professor with no choice but to give you an F. Or you may find yourself thinking one thing but saying something entirely different. For instance, you may tell your family you're flush with money when truly the only way to meet this month's bills is to create an even larger debt load.

Resist the temptation to engage in self-stroking reveries of being smarter, more talented or more creative than others. This kind of fantasizing encourages you to usurp taking action that can help you cultivate your talents. Discrepancies between your 'real self' and your 'dream self' undermine a solid belief in yourself.

Ground Your Thinking by Using the "5 W's & 1 H" Approach.

One of the most effective ways to ground your thinking is to ask relevant questions that begin with: Who, What, Where, When, Why and How. Here's a model to help you get started, based on your amorphous desire to "get rich."

- *Who* would hire me or retain my services?

- *What* talents do I possess that might make me money?

- *Where* could I work that would enable me to reach my goal?

- *When* would I be able to earn what I'd like to earn?

- *Why* do I want to be rich?

- *How* can investments help me reach my goal?

This exercise is designed not only to help you turn a vague dream into a solid step-by-step action plan (although that in itself would be a laudable achievement) but also to prompt you to examine a task from a number of different mindsets. By doing so, you start doing, not just wishing and hoping.

Challenge Yourself to Pay More Attention to Details.

Have you had the experience of learning a new word and then suddenly you seem to see that word everywhere? Of course the word has been there all the time; you just never paid attention to it. Since dreamers tend to focus on the whole and gloss over the details, challenge yourself to be more aware of the details.

To-Do Exercise

Look around you. Without getting up from your seat, notice something you hadn't noticed before. Look with wide-open eyes. Observe either a new object or a new detail about a familiar object.

This exercise works even with your own body. Put your left hand out in front of you. Pretend you're a neurosurgeon specializing in hands. What details do you notice about your own hand that you haven't seen before? Now pretend that you're an artist who is going to paint your hand? What details do you notice now? Now put both hands out in front of you. Notice three differences between your two hands.

Yes, there's always more to observe. As a dreamer, your creativity is your strength; your lack of attention to details is your weakness. Once you begin to notice the details that make up the whole, they'll be no stopping you!

Enriching Your Speaking Skills

Limit Your Use of Vague Phrases.

Notice how you speak about your future. If you're like most dreamers, you probably use an abundance of dreamy words. A few examples:

- "*I wish* I could decide on a color scheme for my project."

- "*I'd like to* lose weight."

- "*I'll try to* finish this project soon."

As you learn to speak more definitively, you'll start acting more definitively. Here are the above sentences just a bit revised.

- "*I will* decide on a color for my renovation project this afternoon."

- "*I am* attending Fat-B-Gone weight loss meetings weekly."

- "*I am* starting this organizational project now and will complete it by tomorrow."

Do you notice the difference in the second set of sentences? As you become more specific about the action you're taking, it becomes natural to articulate a time frame to accomplish the task.

Use Concrete, Active Language.

Notice the subtle ways in which you speak evasively or in generalities. For example, as a way of obscuring your personal responsibility, you might tell a friend:

- "I have a cash flow problem" instead of "I'm in debt."

- "It's a lazy day today" instead of "I feel lazy."

- "I'm getting out of shape" instead of "I am out of shape."

Avoid euphemisms. Speak about 'what is' clearly and accurately. That way, you'll have little opportunity for sidestepping reality. You may initially feel uncomfortable speaking in this precise manner. But give it a shot. It gets to feel more natural with practice. And the perk for you will be a firmer grip on what your situation really is.

Limit Your Use of "Someday," "Soon," and "When I Get a Chance."

Have you noticed that "someday" rarely arrives? That "soon" often morphs into later or never. "When I get a chance"—um, when exactly will that be? Using such fuzzy time-frames easily provides a blanket excuse to let matters drift by. Change that. Rather than saying:

- "I'll organize my desk someday," say "*Today* is the day I'm organizing my desk."

- "I'll complete my report soon," say "I'm finishing my report *this morning.*"

- "When I get a chance, I'll throw it out," say "It's *done!*"

Speaking in fuzzy time frequently puts you on the defensive. Do you really want to be explaining to your boss why you thought "doing it soon" meant sometime this month, while he took it to mean you'd complete it before the end of the day?

Talking about fuzzy phrases, here's another tip. Avoid using the word "it" when "it" is being used to help you duck your accountability. Here's an example: *"It* will be done by next week." That's fine to say if you're speaking about Congress voting on the budget. But if you're speaking about what *you're responsible* for doing, then say, *"I* will get it done by next week."

Avoid Engaging in "Say It and It's True" Talk.

Guard against using grandiose ("say it and it's true") language, such as:

- "I deserve to make more money."

- "I'm entitled to take time off."

- "I shouldn't have to account for my time."

- "I'm the best person for the job."

Though these types of statements may have a grain of truth to them, they may reflect more wishful thinking than reality. When you're tempted to make such self-inflating statements, back them up with facts. When you do, your original statement will probably be rendered less extreme. For example, rather than saying, "I deserve to make more money," clarify *why* you think that's true. You might say, "I deserve a raise because I've created more sales this past quarter than anyone else in the company." Once you base your belief on facts, it's easier to open up a dialogue with the powers that be. If the boss agrees, great; you've made a point and proved it! If he disagrees and explains why, at least you'll gain a clearer understanding of the rules of the game.

Expanding Your Action Skills

Create a Written Plan for *How* and *When* You'll Do Important Tasks.

By writing down the specific milestones and deadlines needed to complete a project, you'll be better equipped to measure your progress. Here's one way to accomplish this:

On the top of the paper or screen, write *the goal* you want to reach *and the date* by which you want to achieve it. Be as specific as possible. "Getting my stuff together" is not nearly as helpful as "Creating a system for organizing my digital and paper files and folders to be completed by February 15th."

On the left-hand side create a time line. Draw a vertical line from top to the bottom. Put today's date at the top of the line and the final goal date at the bottom. In the above example, the final goal date is February 15.

Between today's date and your end date list the major tasks you'll do to achieve your goal. Put a specific time-frame next to each major accomplishment, such as:

- Deleting old unneeded computer files

- Organizing files into folders

- Labeling paper folders

- Organizing your drawers and shelves

Break down large, onerous tasks into more manageable ones. That way, each time you complete even a small task, you'll feel a surge of success, not a frustrating feeling of failure. As you complete small steps, give yourself a pat on the back. Acknowledge that you're on the road to success!

To-Do Exercise

Any advice becomes more effective when you *do it,* not just read about it. Hence, begin now to create your own written plan for achieving one of your goals.

- Pick a goal that's been eluding you

- Write down specific steps you need to do to make this goal a reality

- Create a time line for each of the milestones

- Monitor your progress; reward yourself for staying on track

Use a Calendar to Keep Track of Day-to-Day Responsibilities.

Like many of today's organizational tools, a calendar can be on your computer, cell, digital gizmo or an old-fashioned paper calendar. It matters not what form it takes. It matters a lot whether you utilize it properly—recording appointments and activities, then checking the calendar often to view what's there.

It's a truism that any system can work if *you* work the system. The converse is also true. *No system works if you don't work the system.* So make sure that whatever system you choose—high-tech or low-tech—you make it work for you. I use a calendar book with a weekly view of my activities. It's large, 8.5 x 11 inches, which makes it highly visible, thus easy to locate. There's plenty of space each day to record items in specific time slots. I write down what I need (or want) to do as soon as I commit to it. That could be a work appointment, a social activity, a contact I need to make or a place I want to go. If an activity requires transportation time, I factor that in on my calendar.

Now you choose what type of calendar is best for you. You may need to experiment with it for awhile. But no matter what calendar you choose, view it as your personal professional organizer that's there to help you meet your responsibilities. Check off each item when it's completed. Or, move it over to the next day if there's still work to be done on that project. And don't forget to check out future entries well in advance so you're not taken by surprise by what's coming up.

Create a 'To-do' List *and* a 'Future To-do' List.

Whereas perfectionists tend to create lists that are overly detailed, dreamers usually don't create any or create ones that are more fantasy than reality. What's a fantasy list?

- Become a millionaire in the next 3 years

- Own my own IT business

- Become an award-winning actress

I'm not suggesting that these goals are necessarily out of reach for you. If that's what you want, more power to you. However, they're not going to happen unless you have a grounded 'to-do list' that highlights the steps you'll take to get you from 'A to Z.' You must keep reminding yourself that to attain your ambitions, you must be on top of the details.

Differentiating between 'to-do' lists and 'future to-do' lists will train you to distinguish between tasks you're committed to accomplishing *on a particular day* and those you plan to get to *sometime down the road*. Dreamer procrastinators often let their day-to-day responsibilities drift into the future-to-do category—even when it gets them in hot water.

To-Do Exercise

No time like the present to begin. So let's start right now with this week's lists.

Create your 'to-do' list for the week. Refine each listing so that it's specific, referencing when and what you will do. For example, if an item on the list reads 'return calls,' refine it so it specifically states which calls and when you will make them.

Create your 'future to do' list. Write down tasks you want to tend to in the near future. Though you don't have to be as detailed with this list, it still helps if you describe *some* detail. For example, 'update my website' is not as specific as: 'edit my bio,' 'modify my graphics,' 'add a description of my new product.'

Be Proactive With Your Long-Term Goals.

If you want to be on top of your game, you've got to be proactive. Don't wait for opportunities to drop into your lap. Become, instead, an active participant in creating your own future. Looking-ahead tasks are tasks you need to do *now* so that your future will not be determined by luck or chance. Examples of such tasks are, "visit the human resources office to find out what job opportunities will be opening up," "surf the Web for companies I might want to work for," "research the housing market in the area I'd like to move to."

Get into the habit of doing at least one task each week that will help you achieve your long-term goals. Though it may feel like *more* work, when your aim is to do *less* work, *this* type of work will help you build a successful future.

> *"I find that the harder I work, the more luck I seem to have."*
> ~ **Thomas Jefferson**

Be More Physically Active.

Don't let yourself be seduced into an excess of passive activities. Rather than lounging in bed, smoking a joint or watching TV, get involved in more physically active pursuits.

Challenge yourself to do something daily that breaks a sweat. Because nothing succeeds like success, find an activity that *you like* to do (it doesn't have to be the gym). Take pride in your pastime. As you become more active, you'll be enacting the second part of Newton's first law of motion:

> *"An object at rest tends to stay at rest;*
> *an object in motion tends to stay in motion."*

Next time you're simply sitting and staring into space, remind yourself that you're an object at rest. Until you shift into motion, you'll remain at rest. Discover the motion that makes you come alive, then get going! Using mechanical aids to spur you into action is a good idea. If you've promised yourself you'll begin your graphics art project by noon, set your watch or cell to beep at that time. The mere act of setting the alarm shows you are becoming more time focused and committed to the work at hand.

Motivate Yourself to be More Interactive with Others.

If you're inclined to stay by yourself in your own little insular dream world, make a determined effort to be more interactive with others. Here are a few suggestions to get you started:

- Create or join an interest-focused group (book club, yoga class)

- Speak with others about your current or future plans

- Interview others about how they've reached success

- Connect with social media groups that reflect your field of interest

Ending Exercise

Congratulations Dreamers! You've completed this chapter. Now take a moment to simply relax and breathe calmly. There's so much valuable information in each section. Although you can read it all, you can't absorb it all—not right away. So, review the change program and choose 1, 2, or 3 skills that you will implement this week. Once you've gotten those under your belt, then go back for more. This program is designed to be *a reference* for you. Take in what you can use now. Then next week, when you're ready to incorporate more skills, return to the program and see what's next for you.

Work Your Creativity
then
Savor the Fruits of Your Labor!

CHAPTER 5

THE WORRIER PERSONALITY
...BUT I'M AFRAID TO MAKE A CHANGE!

Welcome Worriers!

YOU HAVE MANY ADMIRABLE QUALITIES. You're careful. You're conscientious. You care. So what's holding you back? Despite your many positive attributes, it's tough for you to take challenges in stride. When confronted with new situations (even attractive ones) you hone in on what might go wrong, glossing over what might go right. So much worrying is not only unproductive, it's also emotionally and physically draining. As playwright William Inge said, "Worry is interest paid on trouble before it becomes due."

In this session, you'll gain a better understanding of your worrier personality—how it helps you and how it handicaps you. But first, take a mini-version of the quiz you took earlier. See which of these questions resonate with you.

- Do I hesitate to leave my "comfort zone," avoiding situations that might make me feel anxious?

- Do I tend to paralyze myself before working on a project by worrying about the "what ifs?"

- Do I maximize problems that might arise while minimizing my ability to deal with such problems?

- Do I have difficulty making decisions, frequently vacillating about what I should do?

- Do I become uptight when an unexpected event disrupts my typical routine?

"Procrastination is like a credit card," chirped comedian Christopher Parker. "It's a lot of fun until you get the bill." Though it may be fun for some, if you're the worrying type you know that it's sheer distress from the scary start until the panicky end. Worrying takes its toll on both your confidence and on your decision-making ability. Even after you make a decision, your worrying is still not over, as you tend to second guess your decisions. What if you made the wrong one?

Being highly alert to the potential problems of a situation, yet blind to its positive potential is no way for you to live. You deserve better. It's time for you to create a new future—one that's less anxious, more adventuresome. Let's begin by taking a look at the stories of two different worrier personalities: Debbie, whose enthusiasm is frozen by fear and David, whose confidence is crushed.

Debbie and David

Debbie, a homemaker and part-time receptionist, freely admits that she's a "bundle of nerves." Her biggest problem, she says, is that "I panic under pressure. It's not like I'm running around screaming; it's that my high stress level incapacitates me. When I'm agitated, I can't focus, can't make a decision and become exhausted from worrying. And sad to say, I haven't accomplished a damn thing!"

Debbie's uneasiness has seeped into many areas of her life, causing her to delay, forgo, or complicate endeavors that could bring her pleasure or self-advancement. For safety's sake, she avoids taking the scary plunge into full-time administrative work that, in calmer moments, she's longed to take. Though she admits to being bored in her current job, she still agonizes over whether she'd be able to deal with what would be expected of her in a new position.

David, a claims manager with a large insurance firm, doesn't view himself as nervous but as stable and prudent. "I try to stay away from work that's too tough. I have to admit, I'm not a risk-taker. I'm more careful and safety-conscious." What David doesn't acknowledge is that underneath his composed surface is a nervous personality. When it's time to make a judgment call (at work or at home), he tends to dodge the issue, suppress his emotions, constrict his actions. Thanks to his safety-conscious inertia, not only is his job in jeopardy, but so is his marriage.

Despite their differences, both Debbie and David display the following personality characteristics:

Highly Resistant to Change

Like Dorothy in The Wizard of Oz, worriers are enthralled by new people and new experiences—in their dreams. Awake, however, their instinct is to head for home. For them, unfamiliar is synonymous with uncomfortable; uncomfortable with intimidating; and intimidating is to be avoided. Even small tasks loom as dormant difficulties. Cleaning out their mess of papers becomes "overwhelming," hence "impossible" to do. Why? Because confronting the mess means making decisions about what to discard, what to file, where to put things.

Worriers yearn for their life to have more exciting experiences and adrenalizing activities. Yet when faced with taking the leap into the unknown, they stay put—choosing safety over adventure. If that means being bored, dissatisfied, or forlorn, so be it; anything's preferable to going out on a limb. Their cautionary mindset is reinforced with a host of "What ifs?" What if I get hurt? What if I fail? What if I make a fool of myself? What if I make the wrong choice? The list is never ending.

As worriers spin an ever-tighter cocoon, it robs them of the opportunity to break out, spread their wings, and fly. We see this in the way Debbie refuses to seriously consider a more demanding, yet interesting job. We also see it in the way David avoids decision making until he has absolutely no choice.

Lack of Confidence in Their Own Abilities

Worriers are terrified at the prospect of doing something "wrong." This doesn't mean anything immoral. Their definition of "wrong" covers a vast territory: it's anything that's inaccurate, inappropriate, unorthodox, uncomfortable or risky.

When their anxiety is high, worriers may shun a project altogether. Or commit to a project, but postpone doing anything about it for as long as they can. Debbie, for example, is always asking for advice even when she knows exactly what she should be doing. While David delays writing a report because he's consumed with angst about how to handle it. Though he calls himself lazy, his primary problem is lack of confidence to make and follow-through on an independent decision.

Making Tentative Commitments

Worriers are ever on guard to hold back or withdraw from making commitments. When they finally do commit, it's often done without the confidence and enthusiasm that ensures success.

For example, Debbie makes a tentative commitment to booking a family vacation. Each time she thinks she's hit upon just the right place, she worries about another aspect of the trip—maybe the weather won't be the best, or the plane fare is so expensive, or the kids will be bored. By worrying about one or another aspect of the trip, she reinforces her fears. Her belief that "nothing is easy" has become a self-fulfilling prophecy. It's no wonder she bemoans the "fact" that "life is terribly hard!"

David depends on his highly structured job to make most of his decisions, just as he relies on his more decisive wife to determine what needs to be done at home. Instead of driving himself through life by his own effort and skill, he coasts along in neutral, oblivious to the problems his indecisiveness creates.

Need Advice and Reassurance from Others

Low self-confidence compels worriers to turn to more confident people for direction and reassurance. In this respect, they're like scared kids, looking for someone to show them the way. Clearly one's family, friends and colleagues can be excellent resources. But it's not their job to function as substitute parents. When worriers rely heavily on others, they put their own growth in peril and jeopardize the integrity of these relationships.

We see this in the way Debbie's always looking for others to tell her how well she handled a situation. This *dependency tendency* is even more apparent in the way David depends on his wife to handle the decisions in their marital life. The price paid is a steep one. It's not only deadlines worriers miss; it's also opportunities, adventures and experience.

To gain a better understanding of how these traits get played out in the life of a worrier personality, let's take a look at Alana's story.

Alana: A Worrier Personality

Alana, an elementary school teacher, arrived for her first coaching session 10 minutes late and very apologetic. "I'm so sorry," she blurted out. "I got lost." She looked frightened, like a kid expecting to be berated. But she settled down as I welcomed her and reassured her that it was okay.

At our initial meeting, Alana told me that her main concern was her passivity. She admitted that she spends a lot of time playing games on her i-Phone, texting friends and commenting on blogs. Though she knew that there was stuff (personal and work-related) that she wanted to accomplish, she just couldn't get herself moving on those things. "I relish the freedom to do what's easy for me. But then I pay a terrible price when I'm faced with a mountain of work. I feel helpless to change. I hope you can figure out what's wrong with me."

In subsequent sessions, Alana came to appreciate that her procrastination involved other issues besides "passivity." She was also seriously lacking in self-confidence, which created an excessive reliance on others. "When I'm unsure about what to do, I want someone to step in and take over," she admitted. "I get so frantic over my obligations that I tend to avoid them." Like most procrastinators, Alana was claiming to be powerless over her tendency to put things off. And like worrier procrastinators, in particular, she was relying on me not only to tell her what this meant, but to fix it for her. Our initial mission was to explore precisely how Alana's worrying hindered her in her daily life. Only then could we devise a specific plan of action for overcoming it.

Procrastinating at Work

When Alana was teaching her third-grade class, her procrastination issues were not so evident. Like most elementary school teachers, she was obliged to structure much of the school day according to a pre-determined, officially sanctioned lesson plan designed to ensure consistency of education for all third-graders. When she was not focused on fulfilling these requirements, she was busy responding to the momentary needs of her students.

Occasionally, however, Alana did encounter a work-related challenge to which she responded in a classic worrier manner. An example: she had been working with a PTA committee whose goal was to create enriched cultural after-school activities for the students. As the representative of the teaching staff, she had taken it upon herself to contact cultural organizations for student programs. Much to her own chagrin, she found herself paralyzed with worry that she'd fail in this endeavor. Hence, she made only a few calls, none of which turned out to be successful. Embarrassed, she didn't own up to her lack of action but simply made an excuse as to why she couldn't show up at future PTA meetings.

A more pervasive problem was her realization that she was in a rut, repeating the same lessons year after year. Though a colleague suggested that she should be more creative with the kids, Alana simply said, she couldn't. It was less frightening for her to repeat the same old stuff than to move beyond her postage-sized comfort zone. Alana fessed up, "I can picture myself becoming a burned-out teacher, just waiting for the day I can retire."

Procrastinating at Home

By the time I met Alana, her troubles had permeated several areas of her life. When feeling ill at ease, she wouldn't just "sit there like a zombie." To relieve the tension, she'd shovel in junk food. The twenty pounds she had recently gained made her feel even worse. To add to her troubles, she was sleeping fitfully through the night, unable to let go of the worries of the day.

This is how Alana described her inner life: "I feel paralyzed when I'm not sure how to approach a task. I don't 'go with the flow' like my friends tell me to. I feel stupid. I envision the worst. I tell myself I should just do whatever I need to do right away because I can't stand working under pressure. Then I drag my heels anyway. It doesn't make sense; I hate pressure yet I keep putting increased pressure on myself!"

Reflecting on her college years, she recalled, "I was a good student, but I was so unsure of myself. I missed out on things I might have enjoyed, if only I could have let myself take a risk.

- I didn't sign up for Russian class because I thought it would be too tough.

- I didn't write for the student magazine because I didn't think my writing would pass muster.

- I didn't participate in a video project because I was anxious about being in the limelight."

I pointed out to Alana how often her actions were chosen with the express purpose of maintaining familiar ways. Even when her ways were not particularly fulfilling, they were predictable, hence safe.

Alana's first years in college were an eye opener for her. "Living on my own was tough," she admitted. "I am the youngest in a large family. I had lots of people to turn to when I was growing up. My mom especially was always there to calm me down so I could do my work. My first semester in college, I was on the phone with her all the time, asking for help. The next semester I called less frequently only because I felt embarrassed; I noticed that none of my friends were calling home so often."

As we worked together, it became clear that Alana displayed a high level of *"anticipatory anxiety."* This is when you experience *more* anxiety *before* an event than when the event actually occurs. Such anxiety is fortified by a never ending cycle of "what ifs":

- What if my work isn't good enough?

- What if I fail?

- What if everyone thinks that what I did is pure crap?

- What if I can't finish the project on time?

Alana's worrying even affected her romantic relationships. Here's a poignant example: "At times I wait so long to make a decision that the decision is made for me. Last year, I met Mike. He was a great guy: confident, strong, secure, decisive and good-looking. Wow, what a combination of traits, I thought; he's perfect for me. But it didn't work out as I had hoped. Instead of making me feel more secure, he began controlling me. I became his puppet. I had no identity, no voice. I knew I had to end the relationship but I didn't know how to do it. I was worried about being alone, with no boyfriend. I kept putting off telling him how I felt. Then I never got a chance. One day, he dumped me, saying I was no fun anymore." By the time I met Alana, she had sworn off dating for the time being. "I still want someone to be close to," she admitted, "but I panic at the thought of having someone dump me again."

Alana's First Steps: Beginning the Change Program

As Alana was mulling over her frustrations, she suddenly cried out, "I'm so sick of my fears." "Congratulations," I replied. "That can be a great motivator." And so it was. After fully appreciating how fed up she was with the way her life was going, Alana was primed for change. We began with a small step that made a huge impact. I taught Alana to approach challenges with a two-step program:

- First: decide if you're ready to commit to a specific action;

- Second: if the answer is "yes," then figure out *how* to accomplish it.

"Yes," Alana heard herself say, "I do want to be more creative with my kids, even if I'm scared to do so." After she made the commitment, she then devoted herself to figuring out *how* she could gain the courage to step outside of her comfort zone. She started with three specific actions: Contact her colleague to hear her ideas on how to be more creative with the kids. Search out a book on "creativity in the classroom." Challenge herself to make her daily lesson plans more creative.

To keep her motivation strong, she compiled a list of short, simple and to-the-point affirmations that encouraged her to stay calm and composed. Here are her favorites: I can do it!—Trust yourself!—Stay calm!

> *"I have not ceased being fearful, but I have ceased to let fear control me. I have accepted fear as a part of life and I've gone ahead despite the pounding in my heart that says turn back, turn back, you'll die if you venture too far."*
>
> ~ **Erica Jong**

Though Alana had never read any of Jong's books, she related right away to the author's philosophy. She was determined not to live the rest of her life controlled by fear. As we worked together, Alana adopted additional approaches to help her live a more expansive life. You can use them, too. Here's how.

THE WORRIER'S CHANGE PROGRAM
Beat Your Procrastination Habit *and* Be Careful and Conscientious

If you scored high on the worrier quiz, you probably noticed an abundance of similarities between Alana's way of living and your own. But you're not Alana. You've got your own history and style of living. Now it's time for you to pull the curtain aside and take a closer look at your story. Take a few moments now to do a self-assessment exercise. Doing so will enable you to gain a deeper appreciation of your own issues. Be one of the 20% of readers who will *do* the exercise, not just skim past it. Remember, the program works if you work the program.

> *"Tell me I'll forget, show me, I may remember, but involve me and I'll understand."*
>
> ~ **Chinese Proverb**

1. Recall an occasion when you shied away from taking appropriate action because of your worries. Reflecting on that situation, ask yourself these questions.

   - What specific worries stopped you from taking action?

   - Looking back on it, do you view that situation now as a missed opportunity? If yes, why?

2. Recall an occasion when you wanted to complete a project but got it done late due to excessive worrying. For that occasion, ask yourself these questions:

   - What were you so worried about?

   - Did your worrying have a positive impact on the project?

   - Were there any consequences for being late? Was your self-esteem tarnished? Were opportunities missed? Were relationships strained?

Congratulations. If you took the time to do the above exercise, you've shown that you're serious about understanding the dynamics of your procrastination. Armed with this understanding, you'll be in a better position to modify your patterns—retaining what works for you, toning down what doesn't. Now, let's delve into specific strategies to help you beat your procrastination habit. Challenge yourself to *deal* with your worries and you'll be amazed at how accomplished you will be!

Guided Imagery for Your Creative Mind

To conquer your tendency to worry, it helps to cultivate an opposing frame of mind: one that is upbeat, confident, and optimistic. The following guided imagery will steer you in that direction. Use it either to overcome a specific worry or as an added dimension to a personal stress reduction program.

To begin, read the visualization slowly until you feel comfortable with its content. Then, either let someone else read you the instructions with a slow, relaxed voice or record these guidelines for your personal use which you can then replay whenever you wish. As you record the guided imagery, be sure to speak in a slow, soothing voice. Pause for thirty seconds between each instruction.

Assume a comfortable position in a place that's quiet, dimly lit, and free from distractions. Some people prefer lying down with their legs straight and slightly apart, their arms extended loosely at their side. Others prefer to sit in a relaxed mode in a comfortable chair, couch or bed.

Close your eyes and take a few deep breaths to clear your mind and relax your body—inhaling s-l-o-w-l-y through your nose, then exhaling s-l-o-w-l-y through your mouth. Let go of any tension or tightness in your body. Allow the thoughts and cares of the day to drift away, leaving your body light, your mind empty.

In this relaxed state, picture yourself standing in a densely wooded forest. You're at the edge of a clearing, slowly looking around. Notice that there are only a few gaps between the trees which make it impossible for you to see far into the forest.

Stand still. Feel yourself become totally motionless, as if you were paralyzed. Though you want to go forward into the forest, *your body refuses to move*. You're aware of how tight your body has become. Feel the increased muscular tension in your arms, legs and torso. Notice that your breathing has become labored.

Now, imagine that you hear a *soft voice* within the forest *gently* calling your name. As it continues to call, your breathing relaxes. Though you're still standing at the edge of the forest, your body feels calmer. You feel safe.

Still relaxed, hear the voice gradually getting louder as it continues to call your name. Suddenly you recognize *that it's your own voice you're hearing but it's stronger and more self-assured.* The voice stops. Then several yards into the forest, you see someone coming toward you. You try to make out who this person is but it's too shadowy to see well.

Imagine this shadowy figure coming closer to the clearing. When it's almost at the edge, *you realize that this figure is you, only looking more confident than you typically look.* Notice what it is about your face and body that appears more confident.

See your confident self stop in front of you. Imagine feeling completely at ease standing face-to-face with both parts of you. Hear your confident self say to you, *"You can move out of your comfort zone. I'll be there to catch you if you fall. I'll be there to show you the way if you are lost."*

Take these words to heart. Savor the hope they give you. Feel confidence rising in your body. Feel warmth spreading from your heart. Then, walk forward into the forest, *knowing that your confident self is there to back you up with support and nurturance.*

As you walk through the forest, see the trees becoming farther apart, letting the sun shine through. You walk until the forest ends, opening up into a meadow. You look up into the clear blue sky, feeling content and proud of yourself. Stay with this feeling as long as you wish. Then slowly open your eyes. Notice how relaxed and calm you feel—in body, mind and spirit. Take time to absorb the meaning of your visualization before you move on to the next section.

Enhancing Your Thinking Skills

Know that Making No Decision *is* a Decision.

Postponing decision-making, then doing nothing, is a decision. If this is your modus operandi, you're placing yourself at the mercy of others and/or at the mercy of fate. Is this your aim? Do you really want others to make decisions for you? Do you really wish to let fate take its course—with no input from you?

If you answered "yes" to any of those questions, it's time for further self-examination. Take a few moments to ponder these questions:

- Why do you think you're incapable of making your own decisions?

- What would happen if you made a decision and it didn't turn out so well?

- If you don't decide things for yourself *now,* when will you?

Don't confuse not making a decision (avoidance) with postponing a decision. Yes, it may be wise for you to:

- Postpone a decision until you have more information

- Postpone a decision until you feel less overwhelmed

- Postpone a decision until you confer with others whose opinion you value

But don't fool yourself into thinking you're postponing a decision if you're really avoiding it.

Reflect on What's Exciting about a Challenge.

There's a fine line between feeling excited and feeling nervous. Worriers are in the habit of leaning toward the nervous side of the line. To counteract this tendency, deliberately lean the other way. Focus on what's exciting, stimulating, or inspiring about a challenge. As you make this shift, you'll discover that worrying and excitement have much in common—the major difference is your interpretation of your bodily experience. So, the next time you have "butterflies in your stomach," try interpreting it as a sign of excitement, not fear.

If this feels counterintuitive to you, take your cue from trapeze artists. Picture yourself high above ground, trying to stay upright as you attempt to keep your balance. Imagine yourself leaning too far to the left. Uh-oh! What do you do? Intuitively, your body knows.

You lean to the right. You feel steadier. Once your body is centered, you begin to move forward again.

If you have difficulty picturing yourself as a trapeze artist, try a different imagery, one even a young child can relate to—learning to ride a bike. At the onset, the skill seems impossible. Someone must help you keep your balance. Or training wheels do the job for you. But then one day, with enough practice, you feel ready. You're a bit wobbly, but so what? That doesn't stop you. You're ready to go. No more training wheels. No more need for an adult to prop you up. You're on your own. And will you succeed? Oh yes, yes indeed. Now, if a child can get excited about a challenge that initially seems impossible, so can you!

Reward Yourself for Taking a Risk.

Having second thoughts about taking a risk? Instead of backtracking and berating yourself (i.e. I must have been crazy to audition for a local "You've Got Talent" group), reward yourself. Remind yourself *why* you initially thought it was a good idea to become involved. Perhaps there's a budding actress inside of you yearning to be free. Even accomplished actresses, like Katherine Hepburn, confessed to being fearful *and* doing it anyway.

> *"Everyone thought I was bold and fearless, even arrogant, but inside I was always quaking."*

If one day in a burst of confidence, you volunteer for the leadership of a "Green Community Project," don't drop the project just because you're feeling flustered about the work. Instead, stay tuned to the full range of benefits this activity can have for you—not the least of which will be an enhanced belief in your abilities. The bottom line: Don't maximize your worries as you minimize your competence. Do just the opposite—maximize your competence as you minimize your worries. That's how you grow a more confident you!

Don't Make Challenges More Intimidating than They are.

Challenges are a part of life. Don't view them as potential disasters. Yes, tough tasks require time, work, effort, concentration and maybe help from others. But who said life was supposed to be easy?

To live up to your potential, guard against your natural tendency to:

- Overestimate the time you'll need to devote to a task

- Overestimate the energy you'll need to expend on a task

- Overestimate unexpected problems that may arise

Instead, make an objective assessment of the challenge you're confronting. You'll be able to tackle much more when you're not weighed down by worries. Feel pride in your accomplishments, joy in your growth. Adopt *"I can do it!"* as your new mantra.

Be Your Own Best Friend by Encouraging and Supporting Yourself.

Your first impulse may be to turn to others for encouragement and support. Good! It's terrific that you have supportive people in your life. But don't let that prevent you from building up your own strong foundation. If you frequently ask friends, family or co-workers how to handle a situation *before* you come up with your own ideas, you're reinforcing your dependency on them. In effect, you're saying, "I can't do this all by myself." Such a statement diminishes your confidence and competence. Certainly it's fine if others are there for you, helping you out *if you need it*. Hence don't cut yourself off from outside help. But do resist the temptation to turn to others *before* you turn to yourself.

To fortify self-reliance, ask yourself these questions:

- What do *I* think would be the best decision?

- What would *I* like to do?

- What resources might *I* explore before making my decision?

- What do *I* already know about this topic?

Asking yourself such questions clarifies your own thinking. Then, if you do seek input from others, you won't come across as weak (i.e. I can't do this) but as strong (i.e. I'd appreciate your input about my ideas).

Encouraging yourself is especially important when you're feeling down. If things haven't gone the way you expected them to, take a sober look at what went wrong. Learn from your mistakes. Cultivate your inner resources. Continue to believe in yourself.

> *"People grow through experience*
> *if they meet life honestly*
> *and courageously. This is*
> *how character is built."*
> **~ Eleanor Roosevelt**

First Commit to the Goal; then Decide How to Achieve it.

If you don't commit to a goal first, it's much harder to figure out how to achieve it. Instead, it's likely you'll just throw your hands up in the air in frustration. For example, if you're not fully committed to getting a graduate degree but only "thinking about it," you'll be easily thrown off course by the first roadblock you hit. And there will be many: additional years in school, high expenses, harsh competition, demanding courses. On the other hand, if you're seriously committed to the goal, you'll find a way to achieve it. Though the path will undoubtedly be filled with obstacles, they won't stop you. If you don't separate these two processes, "hang-ups and bang-ups" will thwart you before you even get out of the starting gate. Listen to the difference between these two statements:

- "I'd like to go to grad school *but* it's so expensive and time consuming."

- "Grad school is so expensive and time consuming *but* it's my paramount goal."

Hear the pessimism in the first sentence, the optimism in the second sentence? Hear the reason why it won't happen in the first sentence, the determination to make it happen in the second sentence? Remember it's what comes *after* the BUT that counts!

Enriching Your Speaking Skills

Reduce the Use of Qualifiers in Your Speech.

Qualifiers are words like, "maybe," "perhaps," "sort of," "kind of," "try to." Qualifiers are used (whether you're aware of it or not) to make tentative statements—ones that dodge firm commitments.

Speak more affirmatively. Instead of saying, *"Maybe* I'll work on my report this week," declare your intentions by saying, "I *will* work on my report this week." To increase your effectiveness, add a definite time-line, "I will start my report on Tuesday, finish it by Friday." Put the kibosh on slippery statements like, "I'll *try to* get to the gym this week." Be precise by saying, "I'm *committed to* getting to the gym on Monday, Wednesday and Friday mornings."

End "I Can't" Statements with "BUT One Thing I Can Do is..."

The phrase "I can't..." (i.e. I can't quit my job now") may leave you feeling hopeless. No choice, no power, no options; you're screwed! Instead of remaining in this powerless position, shift the focus away from what you *can't* do to what you *can* do. For example, you might say, "I can't quit my job now, BUT I can research alternative career moves," or..."BUT I can speak to a head-hunter to explore the job market."

To make your language more upbeat (hence less mired in procrastination), don't end your sentence on a pessimistic note. Aim for an upbeat note that motivates you to take action. Knowing "one thing you can do" provides you with a defined direction to explore options, develop plans, build personal power. Once again, notice that what comes *after* the BUT is what counts.

To-Do Exercise

Now it's time to make this tip particularly relevant to you. Write down your own sentence that begins with *"I can't."* Keep the same sentence and add ...*BUT one thing I can do is....*" Don't skim over this exercise, do it now! Once you expanded your sentence, what did you notice? Did you feel different when you ended on an empowering note? Now, challenge yourself to put this new skill into practice on a regular basis.

End "I Don't Know" Statements with "BUT One Thing I Do Know is..."

Another way of encouraging yourself to become more action prone is to minimize the times you say "I don't know." "I don't know..." is often tossed off casually as a way to avoid confronting a deeper, more revealing assessment of a situation. Though this may seem like a good idea (why visit underlying insecurities), the downside is that you can't find solutions for what you don't directly address.

To become more action-oriented, challenge yourself to explore what you *do* know. Instead of despondently saying, "I don't know why I stay in this awful relationship," say something like, "...BUT one thing I do know is that I'm afraid to be alone." Or, "one thing I do know is that constant conflict is depressing me." Does this solve your problem? No, it does not. Does it create the possibility that owning up to what the problem is might help you find a solution? Yes, it does.

To-Do Exercise

Now, it's time to make this tip more personal. Write down your own sentence that begins with *"I don't know."* Keep the same sentence but add: *"…BUT one thing I do know is…."* Don't skim over this simple exercise, do it now! Once you expanded your sentence, what did you notice? Did you feel different when you ended on an empowering note? Now, challenge yourself to put this new skill into practice on a daily basis.

Answer "What If?" Questions.

Don't fall into the pattern of using rhetorical "what if?" questions to dramatize and justify your inactivity. Suppose, for example, that you delay booking a long-overdue vacation, explaining your shirking behavior by saying, *"What if* I'm tied down with work at that time?" Allowing this statement to remain unanswered not only reinforces your worries, but also seduces a listener to buy into that worry. An alternative approach: Sure it's frustrating that you may be too busy to take a vacation. Inspiration, however, is often born from frustration. Get inspired. Figure out your options, if indeed, you will be busy. Here are a few possibilities.

- Put more energy into your work *now* so that you ensure you'll have time to take a vacation later.

- Work while you're on vacation (hopefully, not so much that it's no vacation at all).

- Review your work load to see what you might be able to delegate.

End "I'm Waiting…" Statements with "Meanwhile, I'm Doing…"

Waiting for something to occur before you take action may seem like a valid excuse for procrastinating. Do any of these examples feel familiar to you?

- *"I'm waiting* to find out what my friend is doing."

- *"I'm waiting* for the monthly sales report."

- *"I'm waiting* until the weekend to do a thorough clean-up."

Don't let "waiting" statements linger around without adding a "meanwhile I'm doing" clause.

- "I'm waiting to find out what my friend is doing, meanwhile, I'm developing possible alternative plans for the weekend."

- "I'm waiting for the monthly sales report; meanwhile, I'm doing the cost-benefit analysis for another project."

- "I'm waiting until the weekend to do a thorough clean-up; meanwhile, I'm tackling this junk drawer right now."

Notice how action-oriented "meanwhile I'm doing" statements are and how passive-oriented "waiting" statements are. Is it truly your preference to wait and worry? Or would you prefer to be more vibrant and vigorous?

Expanding Your Action Skills

Turn Big Intimidating Tasks into Smaller, Less Threatening Ones.

Scratch the habit of overwhelming yourself by looking at the whole panorama of tasks ahead of you. Instead, divide the big panorama of responsibilities into smaller ones. That way, you'll make them less threatening and easier to do.

For a major project, follow this five part strategy:

1. Determine a specific date to have the whole project completed

2. Outline the major steps involved in that project

3. Focus on no more than 1 or 2 steps at a time

4. When you've completed those steps, go on to the next ones

5. Monitor your progress—*I'm 20% done, I'm 40% done, wow I'm 60% done, I'm almost there, yes, I'm done!!!*

An example: You haven't written a resume in more than a decade. And now you're back in the job market. You want to compose a professional looking resume but don't know how to account for the time you've been out of work. Break this daunting task into a number of less complex ones. Here are a few possibilities:

- Search on-line for prototypes of all types of resumes

- Decide which type best fits your needs

- Compile a list of your previous positions

- Jot down descriptions of your skills

- Write a first draft of a resume based on the above

- Revise that draft

- Show your revised draft to someone whose opinion you respect

- Revise the draft again

- Decide if you need professional help to polish up your resume

- Work with a pro to produce the final copy

As you complete each mini-task, celebrate your progress—with yourself and with others who will appreciate what you've accomplished. As you do this, you'll feel more empowered. As you feel more empowered, you'll be more motivated. As you become more motivated, the job gets easier. Why? Because *nothing succeeds like success!*

Develop a Personal Library of 'Get up and Go' Motivational Prods.

Build a motivational library by collecting upbeat quotes, creating uplifting affirmations, buying motivational books, listening to inspirational music. By doing so, you can be your own cheerleader. Three of my favorite quotes for worriers are:

> *"The policy of being too cautious is the greatest risk of all."*
> **~ Jawaharlal Nehru**

> *"He who is not courageous enough to take risks will accomplish nothing in life."*
> **~ Muhammad Ali**

> *"The reason why worry kills more people than work is that more people worry than work."*
> **~ Robert Frost**

Three of my favorite affirmations are:

"You can do it!"
"You're up to the challenge!"
"It'll work out!"

My favorite motivational book for worriers is:

"Oh, the Places You'll Go"—By Dr. Seuss

Yes, this is a kid's book. But it talks to the scared, helpless child inside each one of us. If you've previously read the book, read it again. If you've never read the book, buy, borrow or pilfer it from a kid who doesn't realize the gem he's got in his hands.

My favorite motivational song for worriers is:

"Three Little Birds"—By Bob Marley

Hearing "every little thing's gonna be all right," repetitively reverberating with the Marley beat, makes you believe it's true. A perfect antidote for worriers!

To-Do Exercise

Make a collection of your favorite motivational quotes. Put one on your bathroom mirror, your refrigerator, your screensaver. If you need assistance finding quotes, visit a wonderful website *www. PsychWisdom.com.* (Yup, it's my website. But hey, if you don't think well of your own work, who will?) On the left menu of the home page, click on *"Quotes to Inspire."* First quote is designed for worriers. Here's what Mark Twain had to say:

"Twenty years from now you will be more disappointed by the things you didn't do than by the things you did. So sail away from the safe harbor. Explore. Dream."

Don't stop with quotes. Collect self-help books. As a worrier, you might want to check out one of my books: *Master Your Fears: How to Triumph over Your Worries and Get on with Your Life* (Wiley, 2004).

Download your favorite motivational songs. Listen to them frequently. Let your body move with the beat. Start your day in the shower singing one of these songs. Music has the ability to alter your mood, diminish your worries. Use it!

Spend More Time with Optimistic Friends.

Although it's a good idea to strengthen your own decision-making ability, there will be times when you'll benefit from receiving advice, support, and reassurance from others. When you do, make sure you're turning to the right people.

Seeking support from a friend who is optimistic can inspire you. Seeking support from a friend who is doom and gloom can leave you feeling dispirited, disheartened, demoralized. So, make sure your friends are upbeat, nurturing people. And whenever those pessimistic folks come knockin' at your door, make their visit short. As you cultivate more positive relationships, let their confidence and enthusiasm rub off on you. Then start weaning yourself off any reliance you have on the pessimists. You don't need them to amplify the worries in your life.

Challenge Yourself to Do what You're Uncomfortable Doing.

You're not going to get better at anything if you keep avoiding it. So, expand your comfort zone by engaging in a broader range of activities, even if you do them awkwardly. Each activity does not have to be a major triumph. An accumulation of small work-outs can create hefty muscles.

The more you avoid tackling a task, the larger it looms. Here are a few examples of pursuits that worriers tend to avoid:

- Discussing a sensitive topic

- Speaking in front of large groups

- Openly disagreeing with a group decision

- Admitting that you don't understand something

- Attempting a new sport or tech program

- Being more assertive in the workplace

- Traveling to a new place

Don't let comfort be your primary concern. You can be uncomfortable AND do it anyway!

To-Do Exercise

Add four more items to the list above. Every week, make it your goal to do one of those activities. Don't wait for a pressured situation. Make it happen now. Often it helps to do something spontaneously; that way you don't have time to talk yourself out of it. For example, suppose you're upset with a friend who frequently undermines what you say. You've wanted to confront her on this for the longest time. Yet, when you think about confronting her, fear weakens your resolve. Next time rather than plan it, just let it happen. Doing something out of character helps you grow your character. Heed the wisdom of Eleanor Roosevelt, when she said:

> *"We gain strength and courage and confidence by each experience in which we really stop to look fear in the face."*

Make it a Priority to Catch Up on Tasks You've been Putting Off.

It's not only onerous tasks that worriers put off doing; it's also activities that you *want to* do but somehow never get around to. So, start catching up on unfinished business by doing at least one task a week that you're not crazy about as well as one task a week that you know you'll enjoy.

The task you choose needn't be a big, complicated, fearsome one. It could be something small but significant like re-connecting with an old friend or organizing your photo folder. You might even do something just for fun that you haven't done for weeks—such as play the piano, sketch a picture or take a stroll around the neighborhood. Don't judge yourself on how well you do these things, just do them. The point is to be able to say to yourself, *"I did it!"*

Ending Exercise

Congratulations Worriers! You've completed this chapter. Now take a moment to simply relax and breathe calmly. There's so much valuable information in each section. Although you can read it all, you can't absorb it all—not right away. So, review the change program and choose 1, 2, or 3 skills that you will implement this week. Once you've gotten those under your belt, then you can go back for more. This program is designed to be a *reference* for you. Take in what you can use now. Then next week, when you're ready to incorporate more skills, return to the program and see what's next for you.

Burst through the Barrier of Worrying
then
Embrace A More Adventurous Life!

CHAPTER 6

THE CRISIS-MAKER PERSONALITY
...BUT I CAN'T GET MOTIVATED UNTIL THE LAST MINUTE!

Welcome Crisis-Makers!

YOU HAVE MANY REMARKABLE QUALITIES. You respond well in an emergency. You thrive on excitement. You enjoy taking risks. So what could be wrong? Here's the problem. You not only *weather* crises well but you're also *responsible for creating* many of those crises in the first place. In those quiet moments of self-reflection, can you really take pride in your achievement when, despite last minute scrambling, you fail to measure up to what you're truly capable of?

I'm sure you know that waiting to act until you're under the gun is *not* the most efficient or effective way to produce quality work. In this chapter, you'll gain a deeper understanding of your crisis-maker personality—how it helps you and how it handicaps you. But first, take a mini-version of the quiz you took earlier. See which of these questions resonate with you.

- Do I ignore attending to important tasks then, at the last minute, work frantically to get them done?

- Do I enjoy taking risks and love the thrill of living on the edge?

- Do my moods tend to change quickly and dramatically?

- Do I have a tendency to get involved with a project, then abruptly detach myself and move on to something else?

- Do I have little patience for activities that are slow, predictable or safe, preferring instead quick, action-oriented projects?

"I work best under pressure" is the battle cry of the crisis-maker procrastinator. Some proclaim it proudly, intimating that they have special last minute rush-to-the-rescue capabilities that make them unique. Others utter it sheepishly, realizing that any skill they have in coping with an emergency is not so much a special ability but a necessary evil, generated by creating the havoc in the first place. Both types of crisis-makers—the proud and the sheepish—are addicted to the adrenaline rush of doing things at the last moment. Until they experience that rush, it's tough for them to get off their butts and tend to what needs to be done.

Many crisis-makers describe their lives as a rollercoaster ride: First, they sit back, allowing a potential predicament to escalate. Then they're jerked into the scary, stimulating highs of adventure only to fall back once again into dreary inaction. Typical crisis-makers have two operating modes: burying their head in the sand and working frenetically when under the gun. They tell themselves they have no control over this pattern, and, indeed as time goes on, that may become a self-fulfilling prophecy.

Why then do crisis-makers take action only when there's a blazing fire to put out? The short answer: because their feelings in the moment are of utmost importance. If they don't *feel* like doing something, they won't. If they *feel* an undertaking isn't to their liking, they won't reflect on why it still may be a good idea to do it. Hence, it's not unusual for crisis-makers to delay completing critical projects, taking care of crucial matters, tending to relationship issues and more.

Let's now take a look at the stories of two types of crisis-makers: the boastful and the mortified.

Scott and Stephanie

Scott, a Wall Street trader, boasts about his crisis-maker lifestyle. He's a great example of the over-stimulated, thrill-seeking dimension of this behavioral pattern. His favorite motto: "You only live once." Exciting adventures enliven him; mundane tasks bore him to death. He relishes the challenge of doing things at the last minute. At those moments, he feels important, even heroic.

If Scott has an appointment to meet friends, he thinks nothing of being a good hour late. Even if he needs to catch a plane, he plays a 'seat of the pants' action game—waiting to leave until the last minute, gambling that the traffic lights will be in his favor. "I play a game with myself," he admits. "Either I get there in record time or curse myself out because I've blown it. There are moments when I think, what am I doing? This is dumb. But it makes my life more captivating. And it avoids what I detest—being bored."

Of course, one reason why Scott feels the need to perform such heroic stunts is that he spends so much of his time in a non-productive manner. He tells himself that he wants to take care of his responsibilities as swiftly as possible, yet paradoxically, he wastes huge blocks of time distracted by digital games. Comparing himself to his better organized girlfriend, he insists, "I admire her ways but I could never be like her. She's predictable and orderly. That's not me!" Scott attributes his pattern to a lack of will power. That's undoubtedly true. But underlying his lack of will power is an addiction to a crisis-maker way of life. For years now, he's let the heat of an emergency be his major motivator.

Stephanie, a student of fashion design, has developed a similar pattern but she's not boastful about it. Instead, she's down on herself, acknowledging how often her procrastination has resulted in lost opportunities and frustrated relationships.

Stephie was raised in an alcoholic family. As a result, she feels that she's never had much control over her life. She sees herself as a scatterbrain doomed to be out of sync with the world. She can't help delaying, ignoring, or even totally forgetting what she was "going to do" until the last possible minute. Then she becomes hysterical, running around frantically, trying to get it all done. "I know I'm not a good planner," Stephie admits. "I dawdle until something dramatic makes me pay attention. When it's crunch time, I feel frazzled. But that seems to be the only time I get stuff done."

Stephie recognizes how debilitating her pattern is but she believes that's just the way she's built; nothing will ever change for her. Like Scott, her crisis-maker pattern pervades many areas of her life. It's not unusual for her to put off deciding what she should wear to an important occasion. Describing one such moment, she said, "I was frantically searching through my closet. I threw together one outfit, yanked it on, yanked it off and went on to the next one. After ten minutes, my room looked like a bomb hit it. I felt like a wild woman. Finally I started screaming in frustration. My room-mate shocked me when she said. 'You're totally out-of-control! You need to get help!' She's right, of course. But I don't know if I can change." Stephie is capable of changing. And she doesn't have to get on meds. Or sign up for a total makeover. What she does need is to learn strategies and skills that will enable her to respond in a more modulated manner.

Though Scott and Stephanie have different lifestyles, they both illustrate the on-off energy pattern of crisis-makers—an adrenaline-charged high followed by a lethargic low. Now let's look at other traits that crisis-makers share:

Believing They Must Get Hyped about a Task *before* They Do It

Waiting until the last minute is a crisis-makers' preferred way to prime the motivation pump. This is especially true when confronted with a task for which they have no intrinsic interest. And let's face it; that includes many work and household chores. They claim—without one iota of logic—that there's no need to get going early on; there's plenty of time to do it all. So they let things go. Then when the crisis is almost at its peak, they jump into action with a burst of energy that gets it all done.

Scott, for example, approaches his work as a game. He can't see any point in filing his tax returns or expense reports until a deadline is staring him in the face. Stephie simply doesn't plan much. She counts on last minute panic to provide the momentum she needs to carry her through. Since pandemonium was a daily occurrence in her childhood, she's accustomed to it—viewing frequent turmoil simply as a way of life.

Difficulty Attending to Tasks on a Routine Schedule

It seems almost impossible for crisis-makers to respond to every-day responsibilities in a thoughtful, practical, and efficient manner. Without an immediate crisis, calls for their time and energy go unheard, unseen, and unaddressed. No crisis, no need to do anything about it. When others urge them to act with more immediacy, their retort may be testy.

We see this characteristic in Scott's insistence that he could never be like his better organized girlfriend. He's convinced that what works for her would simply be too tedious for him—even though he's never given it a fair trial. Stephie also maintains that she can't live a less frenetic life, despite the fact that her turbulent existence makes her miserable. It's as if she's afraid that without a crisis to stimulate her, she'd be left in a state of emotional lethargy. She's unaware that the two states of crisis and lethargy are codependent, and that an entirely different state of well-balanced efficiency would be preferable to either one of them.

Over-dramatizing Situations

Crisis-makers are drawn toward the theatrical. And procrastination provides them with all the dramatic elements they'll ever need. It creates conflict: the hero is challenged with a near impossible task. It builds suspense: will the hero get the task done? And it guarantees a thrilling climax: a victory against all odds or horrendous defeat.

Scott represents the fully flamboyant hero. He deliberately courts disaster by letting things go till the last minute—not only as a way of making life more riveting to him but also as a way of making him more riveting to others. We can imagine his friends sitting in that restaurant waiting for him to make his grand entrance, wondering: will he ever get here; did something happen to him; is he making a last minute dash once again?

Stephie is not trying to be a hero by procrastinating, but it does provide a way for her to routinely get attention. Consider, for example, the time she was trying on outfits for an interview. She wound up crying out in frustration, a signal for her roommate to enter the scene. Her roommate not only calmed her down, but provided a summation of her performance!

Feeling Fully Alive by Living on the Edge

Beneath the crisis maker's sensational theatrics lay feelings of emptiness. To counteract this emptiness, they court attention and recognition via high drama scenarios. How to stir up such drama? Repeatedly procrastinating is one obvious way. By putting themselves at risk in this manner, they shock themselves—not only into *doing* something—but also into *being* someone. Not just an ordinary person but the central figure in a drama.

Scott exhibits this characteristic by delaying mundane matters—until he can do it heroically, that is, in the fastest time it can be done. It's a big crap shoot but it's the only way he knows to jump-start his engine. Crises enable Stephie to escape her emptiness with a frenzy of self display. She runs around, becomes hysterical, and screams for help. Instead of being a hopeless non-entity with no control over her life, she loops into being a self-declared "wild woman!"

Scott and Stephie possess all the above traits of a crisis-maker personality. In style, however, they're on opposite ends of the spectrum: Scott boasts about the label, while Stephie's embarrassed, even ashamed of it. Now, let's examine in greater detail a crisis-maker whose pattern falls in the middle of the spectrum.

Michael: A Crisis-Maker Personality

Michael, a partner in a high-powered law firm, introduced himself to me as an "eleventh hour specialist." "I like that moniker," he said lightheartedly. Yet, it wasn't long before his tone changed. "It used to be exciting to wait until the last minute to get it all done. I imagined myself to be a heroic figure stepping in at the last minute to rescue all from disaster. But now, it's just tiring. I no longer get the kick out of it that I used to. Though I confess, I still function with a wait-and-do operating system."

When I asked Mike to describe his wait-and-do operating system, he responded, "Inspiration only arrives when I have a significant objective staring me in the face. Otherwise, I say, why bother? Once I'm in the zone, however, I'm on a mission! A wave of energy courses through my body. I am confident; I am competent. And I get it all done." "Mike," I inquired, "what it's like for you *before* you're in the zone?" He shrugged, "I don't feel much of anything. Yeah, there's work to be done but I can't bring myself to care about it. I'm more interested in adventure games or gambling online. You name it; any alternative seems more desirable."

Mike admitted that his moods can change dramatically—from the high of being in the zone to the apathy of not giving a damn. This emotional seesaw was his primary motivation for seeking coaching. "Lately, it's tough for me to swing into action when I need to," he fessed up. "Pulling an all-nighter is not the same as it was in college. Now I'm wiped out the next day. And my self-esteem is in the toilet because I know I screwed up once again."

Procrastinating at Work

Though Mike considers himself to be an ethical attorney, nevertheless, he repeatedly courts disaster by letting calls, reports, and filings wait until the last moment. To save his own reputation, once he's on a roll, he feels compelled to work himself and his associates hard. Understandably, such episodes generate friction between Mike and his staff.

Spurred by a looming deadline, they all need to go into "work overdrive" to avert a crisis. To Mike, this way of working has been a source of pride. He interprets the team effort as one that "brings out the best in us." His staff, however, views the situation quite differently. To them, it's an unnecessary rush job that threatens their morale, intrudes on their personal time, and gives rise to resentment. They're well aware that if only he had paced his activities from the start, there'd be no crisis to deal with now.

When a disgruntled staff member confronts him on his crisis-maker style, Mike distorts details to conform to his interpretation of the facts. For example, if June 1 was the due date for a filing, Mike would consider the real due date to be June 30, the last day of a 30-day grace period. Mike was so accustomed to believing that you *don't have* to do a task until zero hour that he came to believe that it was absurd to do it until then.

When Mike can't justify his delaying tactics, he resorts to the most primitive defense mechanism—denial. "If I'm late addressing an obligation, I may end up acting as though it doesn't exist," Mike divulged. "That's when I enter my 'oh well, whatever' mode. Yes, I know I should be more concerned that I may mess matters up, but it's hard for me to hone in on what I don't want to do. I was diagnosed with ADD in high school. So, I've been operating on a wait-till-the-last-minute mode forever."

Procrastinating at Home

As undisciplined as he is at work, Mike is even more inclined to indulge his natural inclination to put things off at home. His wife has felt victimized by his 'on again-off again' character for so long that she's lost respect for him. She now looks upon him as a somewhat hopeless character who can't be counted on. She berates him for operating on "Mike time," which she describes as being busy with all his tech stuff but with no specific goal in mind until crunch time, when he goes into a frenzy of activity. At that time, if someone gets in his way, God help them. Mike has a different take on his pattern. "Some things are just boring; I can't get into them. Yet, when I'm down to the wire, I respond in a hyper-charged way. I've done this my whole life. I don't know if I can change the pattern."

Mike's crisis-making personality has inflicted serious emotional damage on his family, something he wasn't initially aware of. Instead of regularly devoting time and energy to family matters, he'd ignore dealing with them until a major problem erupted. An example: shortly before I met Mike, his son was caught smoking pot in school and was put on probation. Mike seized upon this occasion as a time for finally getting closer to his son, only to discover that Jason had long been hardened against him. With anguish, he said, "I always meant to spend more time with him, but I didn't. Then he just wasn't around anymore. I hadn't really noticed how distant he had become. "

Faced with this alienation at home, Mike was filled with regret. "My family is so important to me, even though I know I don't always show it. I couldn't make it if it weren't for them. My wife takes care of so much. And she knows how to prod me into getting things done when I have trouble motivating myself. I hope I haven't lost my wife's respect."

At this stage in his life, Mike recognized that his procrastination was simply too risky for him to dismiss with a shrug and a cocky retort. He was primed for change.

> *"Inspiration is for amateurs. The rest of us just show up and get to work."*
>
> **~ Chuck Close**

Michael's First Steps: Beginning the Change Program

I suggested to Michael that he kick off his change program by toning down his highly dramatic language. When faced with a task he didn't like, he would typically describe it with odious language, such as "it's loathsome" or "it's ridiculously tedious and tiresome." Such speech reflected and reinforced his behavioral pattern of remaining sluggishly inactive until crunch time. Rather than using such intense words for dramatic effect, Mike learned to use more temperate language to describe an onerous task. As we worked together, Mike adopted other easy-to-learn techniques to overcome his crisis-maker inclinations. You can use them, too. Here's how.

THE CRISIS-MAKER'S CHANGE PROGRAM
How to Beat Your Procrastination Habit *and* Live a Feisty Life

If you scored high on the crisis-maker quiz, you probably noticed an abundance of similarities between Mike's procrastination patterns and your own. But you are not Mike. You've got your own history and style of living. Now it's time for you to pull the curtain aside and take a closer look at your story. Take a few moments to do a self-assessment exercise. Doing so will enable you to gain a deeper appreciation of your own issues. Be one of the 20% of readers who will *do* the exercise, not just skim through it.

> *"Tell me I'll forget, show me,*
> *I may remember, but involve*
> *me and I'll understand."*
> ~ **Chinese Proverb**

1. Recall an occasion when you avoided doing a task because the prospect of working on it seemed to be such a drag. Reflecting on that occasion, ask yourself these questions:

    • What specifically seemed to be such a drag?

    • What were the consequences of your dragging your heels on this particular project?

    • Do you reflect on it now as a missed opportunity? If yes, why?

2. Recall a time when you finished a task but got it done late because you waited until a crisis forced you to act. Now ask yourself:

    • What steps could you have taken to avert the crisis?

    • Were there any consequences for being late? Was your self-esteem tarnished? Were opportunities missed? Were relationships strained?

Congratulations! If you took the time to do the above exercise, you've shown that you're serious about understanding the dynamics of your procrastination. Armed with this understanding, you'll be in a better position to modify your patterns—retaining what works for you, toning down what doesn't. Now let's delve into specific strategies to help you beat your procrastination pattern.

Guided Imagery for Your Creative Mind

If you're caught up in a habitual cycle of excitement and collapse, you may rarely experience genuine peace of mind. Guided imagery will help you appreciate how amazingly alive you can feel when you're not in the midst of such turmoil. The following guided imagery will enable you to feel the difference between the "exhausting" experience of sensory overload and the "enlivening" experience of sensory balance.

To begin, read the visualization slowly until you feel comfortable with its content. Then, either let someone else read you the instructions with a slow, relaxed voice or record these guidelines for your personal use which you can then replay whenever you wish. As you record the guided imagery, be sure to speak in a slow, soothing voice. Pause for thirty seconds between each instruction.

Assume a comfortable position in a place that is quiet, dimly lit, and free from distractions. Some people prefer lying down with their legs straight and slightly apart, their arms extended loosely at their side. Others prefer to sit in a relaxed mode in a comfortable chair, couch or bed.

Close your eyes and take a few deep breaths to clear your mind and relax your body—inhaling s-l-o-w-l-y through your nose, exhaling s-l-o-w-l-y through your mouth. Let go of any tension or tightness in your body. Allow the thoughts and cares of the day to drift away, leaving your body light, your mind empty.

As you resume normal breathing, *imagine that you are standing in complete and silent darkness.* You can't see, hear, smell, touch, or taste anything. Feel yourself getting nervous about what might happen next.

Suddenly, a light switches on. You find yourself standing in a room, *surrounded by people who are making demands on you.* You run from person to person, noticing how upset each one is with you. You hear their voices insisting that you do something *right now.* It all feels so chaotic. Notice that the tension in your body has dramatically increased.

In the midst of the chaos, you *notice a light switch on the wall.* Imagine yourself turning the switch "off" and being plunged, once again, into total darkness and silence.

After a few moments, you notice an object radiating light a few feet ahead of you. See it continue to glow in the dark until you can make out that the object is a cozy, comfortable couch. Hear a gentle voice saying, *"Sit down and relax. You're going to be soothed in all your five senses."* You listen. Though you're nervous, you trust what the voice is telling you.

As you sit comfortably in the darkness, you hear *soft, sweet music.* It reminds you of bird songs and the bubbling of springtime streams. It's the most soothing music you've ever heard. As you continue listening, *you feel a sense of peace alight upon you.*

See the darkness around you start to lift. Now you can see a beautiful meadow in front of you, with colorful flowers, waving grasses, and small groves of trees. It's a bright sunny day. *The blue sky has a few white clouds sailing across it.*

The fresh air smells delightful and feels refreshing as it lightly caresses your body. Gently touch your hands to your face. *Feel the warmth of your hands caressing your skin.* Feel at peace with yourself and with the world.

Still relaxing, notice how hungry you're feeling. Look to your right and see a small table that's holding three of your favorite foods. *Savor the taste and smell of these foods.* Notice that they taste even more delicious than usual. Enjoy the moment. Satiate your hunger until you feel pleasantly full.

As you sink down into the couch, notice how fully alive you feel. As you continue to luxuriate in your newly charged senses, hear that gentle voice saying, *"When you work without chaos swirling around you, you will feel an inner sense of well-being."*

Continue to relax, taking comfort in the words you've just heard. Then, whenever you're ready, slowly open your eyes. Take time to absorb the meaning of your visualization before you move on to the next section.

Enhancing Your Thinking Skills

Identify Other Reasons to Take Action besides Last Minute Stress.

Some people think of stress in negative terms (i.e. anxiety, pressure, tension). However, stress can also be experienced in a positive way (i.e. excitement, passion, curiosity). Hence, the goal is not to avoid stress but to increase the excitement, passion and curiosity you feel as you go about your daily activities.

To accomplish this, develop a variety of potential motivators. Here's a list of 10 questions to ask yourself when you're tempted to put off doing a task. Will doing this task:

- Enhance my personal sense of accomplishment?

- Enrich my career prospects?

- Strengthen my physical, emotional, or mental wellbeing?

- Improve my relationship with others?

- Develop my independence and maturity?

- Help me feel better about myself?

- Give me more time to do other things I care about?

- Benefit me financially?

- Allow me to meet my ethical responsibilities?

- Satisfy my curiosity about the topic?

> *"At a child's birth, if a mother could ask a fairy godmother to endow it with the most useful gift, that gift would be curiosity."*
> **~ Eleanor Roosevelt**

To-Do Exercise

Reread the 10 questions. Elaborate on your answers to at least 5 of them. See how your answers can motivate you to get going when you're tempted to procrastinate. Entitle your essay:

Reasons to Do a Task Even if I Don't Feel Like it.

Know that Interest in a Task may not Develop until *After* you've Started Doing it.

You may be quick to assume that a task isn't worth doing if it fails to intrigue you right away. This type of thinking insists that an activity must lure you into action. Drop this passive approach! Instead, coach yourself into adopting a proactive, upbeat frame of reference. Rather than thinking:

"A task has to interest me before I get myself involved in it,"

think

"I have to get myself involved in a task before it interests me."

Often, it's the first few minutes of doing a task that's the major obstacle. Little kids typically don't want to take a bath, but once they're in the tub, they don't want to get out. Adults often don't want to go to the gym. Then once they're there, they feel energized and wonder what all the resistance was about. So, instead of letting your whims, distractions, seductions and, ultimately, emergencies decide what you'll do, let your executive self (the smart part of your brain) drive your decisions.

Focus More on the Facts, Less on Your Feelings.

As a crisis-maker, you're inclined to put more emphasis on how you feel, less emphasis on what you know. Feelings are important, of course, but so are thoughts. Hence, strive to maintain a viable balance between the two. Shift your focus away from resisting (a passive point of view); focus instead on accomplishing (an active point of view).

As you focus on the facts, you'll notice that your assumptions will have a better chance of meshing up with reality. Here's how a crisis-maker might make a false assumption based on what he *wants* it to be rather than on 'what is.'

- My taxes are due on the 15th (a fact) but it won't make a difference if I'm just a few weeks late (a false assumption).

- The engine light on my car is blinking (a fact), but it's the light that's broken (a false assumption).

> *"We do not deal so much*
> *in facts when we are*
> *contemplating ourselves."*
> ~ Mark Twain

To-Do Exercise

Think of a specific task you've been putting off. Then answer these questions in writing.

- How can I make this task more enjoyable, less burdensome?

- What part of the task could I begin to do *now?* (It often helps to begin with the most interesting part of the project.)

- What will be the most likely outcome if I continue to delay doing this task?

- How will I feel about *myself* next week if I don't take action *now?*

What did you learn from this exercise? What will stick in your mind next time you're inclined to procrastinate?

Think more Moderately.

Resist your tendency to make responsibilities more onerous by thinking about them in an exaggerated manner. Examples of such thoughts are:

- "I've got a zillion things to do this week."

- "I'm so busy I can't see straight."

- "My boss expects too much of me."

Focus on clarifying and moderating the situation by asking yourself questions such as:

- What are all these "zillion things" I have to do this week?

- What could I do to at least get my feet wet on one of the tasks?

- How can I give myself time and space to "see straight?"

- How can I deal with one thing at a time?

- How can I perceive my obligations as less overwhelming?

Enriching Your Speaking Skills

Stop Speaking about Yourself as a Victim.

No, you're not a helpless victim. Sure there are some aspects of your life that you're not in control of. You didn't expect to get a serious illness, a financial reversal, a divorce, a kid on drugs. Other situations may be less serious but just as frustrating. You're working at a job you dislike; you and your spouse are arguing; your kids are having difficulties in school. In short, life has not turned out the way you expected it to.

So what are you going to do about it? Be a victim? Constantly complain? Wallow in misery? Or, are you going to figure out where your power lies. Maybe you need to try family therapy, change jobs, brace yourself for chemo. You haven't received a life sentence in prison (I hope). But, it might be that you're in the wrong marriage, wrong career, wrong company, wrong neighborhood. Reflect on the matter. Pinpoint the problem. Then make a decision as to how you'll grow your future. If, on the other hand, you stay in the position of "I have no choice," you reinforce a powerless, ineffectual mind-set. And if you don't do anything about changing that now, what makes you think it'll be any different in the future?

To-Do Exercise

Think of a situation in which you view yourself as a victim. If you're thinking about skipping this exercise by saying, "This is dumb" or "I can't do this," you're actually enacting the victim position. So instead of complaining, do it!

As you reflect on this situation, discover where your power lies. The answer may not come to you right away but stay with it. In *every* situation, you've got power. Don't believe me? Listen to Viktor Frankel, a World War II concentration camp survivor:

> *"The one thing you can't take away from me is the way*
> *I choose to respond to what you do to me."*

Speak about the Positive Aspects of a Task.

Not only do you need to avoid speaking about yourself as a victim, you also need to avoid badmouthing your responsibilities. Sure, it may be tempting to talk as though you and your responsibilities are always in disaster mode. It may even be true, but it's definitely not helpful!

For example, if you need to fill out a mortgage application, you may hone in on *"how long, difficult, intrusive, annoying and time-consuming"* the task is. This may all be true. But if you remain stuck in that negative position, it will increase the likelihood that you'll slack off completing the application. Keep on telling yourself how much you hate "this stupid form" and you're on the road to creating one more crisis of your own making.

I'm not advocating lying to yourself about your feelings. If you really don't like a task, you don't like it. Expressing the negative is okay provided you follow up with an action-oriented, upbeat ending to your sentence. Let's look at how this might sound using the above example:

> *"The mortgage application is long, difficult, intrusive,*
> *annoying and time-consuming, AND once I complete it,*
> *I'll be that much closer to buying my dream house."*

As you develop a habit of ending your sentence on an upbeat note, you may even arrive at the point where you skip right to the action-oriented part, passing over the negative because you view it as just not that important.

Use More Action-oriented Words, Less Feeling Words.

Minimize your use of feeling words, particularly those that turn you off to work, such as:

- I hate…

- I don't feel like…

- I don't care about...

- I'm too lazy to...

Substitute action words like:

- I'm organizing...

- I'm doing...

- I'm scheduling...

- I'm completing...

Don't for one moment think I want to turn you into a robotic nerd. Of course, you can express your feelings; just don't let those feelings impede you from reaching your goals.

Minimize Overly Dramatic Language.

You may notice that you often describe events with extreme language—from "the best ever" at one end of the spectrum to "dreadfully awful" at the other end. To counteract this tendency, use more temperate words. If you liked a task, speak about it as "enjoyable." If you disliked it, speak about it as "not my thing." Using less extreme language moderates your mind-set, preparing you to take action for all kinds of activity. For example, instead of saying:

"Writing that speech today was a total turn-off; I detested it."

say

"Writing that speech was tough,
but I'm hoping my hard work will pay off in the end."

I'm not suggesting you eliminate over-the-top words from your vocabulary. But do save them for over-the-top experiences.

Expanding Your Action Skills

Keep a Log of Repetitive Crises in Your Life.

I know—it's a pain to keep a journal. But it would be helpful for you to become more aware of *when and why* repetitive crises in your life keep popping up. So, keep your journal simple. Record it in an online document, jotting down those occasions when:

- You failed to address a potentially problematic situation until it became a crisis.

- You didn't take care of a responsibility when you said you would.

- You wasted time doing nothing productive or even enjoyable.

Record the time and date for each incident, including statements about:

- Your procrastination trigger (i.e. hangover, bad mood, lethargy)

- What finally got you going (i.e. spouse's anger, zero hour)

- False assumption you harbored (i.e. wrong due date)

Notice that keeping a journal points you in the direction of an action, solution-oriented approach and turns you away from a victim, complaint-oriented approach. That in itself is helpful!

Create Action Plans to Deal with the Crises in Your Journal.

After a month of keeping the journal, review what you wrote. See if there's a pattern to it. Here's what one crisis-maker noticed: "I have a tough time getting motivated in the morning because I feel so lethargic." Once you're aware of a pattern to your procrastination, take steps to counteract it. If you know that you have difficulty getting revved up in the early hours of the day, start the morning with no other goal than to get your motor running. Try:

- 10 stretches before you hop in the shower

- 10 minute jog to get energized

- 10 minute clean-up campaign of your personal space

If you know that you have trouble staying on task when others are present, strive to create a less distractible environment. Try:

- Creating quiet time during your day to focus on your tasks

- Staying up late if you need time alone without any distractions

- Turning your gadgets and gizmos off for a set period of time

By now, you know that no system works unless you work the system. There's no one right action plan. Experiment with alternative behaviors and use what works for you.

Invent a Game to Motivate You to Do a Boring Task.

Any task can be made more interesting simply by turning it into a game. Assuming you've got a playful nature, as many crisis makers do, capitalize on it instead of repeatedly letting it get you into trouble. Make a contest out of a task that seems too dreary to do. Challenge yourself to find a compelling way of doing your chore.

Some playful crisis-makers stage their own personal version of "Beat the Clock," an old-time TV game show. In this show, the contestants were directed to do some ridiculous task as fast as they could. An example: carrying five eggs on a spoon from one end of the stage to the other, while wearing boxing gloves and skipping. An enormous clock face showed the minutes clicking down to the deadline. You can apply a similar, though less preposterous game toward completing a task you find oh, so boring.

If you want to clean your kitchen but can't motivate yourself to get going, set a timer for 15 minutes. Then rush around doing as much as you can within that period of time, making sure that the most important things get done. When the timer goes off, stop and look around. You'll be amazed at how much you accomplished in a short period of time.

Or, play a game with yourself by creating a false deadline date. Yes, that's right. Instead of believing that crunch time for income tax filing is April 15th, make it April 5th. Shrink the time available to do the job and notice your motivation peak. This trick will not only gratify you; it will astonish all others!

> "In every job that must be done, there is an element of fun. You find the fun and...SNAP! The job's a game!"
>
> ~ Julie Andrews

Get Involved in Adrenaline-flowing Activities.

If you need that adrenaline rush to get yourself going, don't just sit there waiting for a crisis to develop. Instead, set up exciting things to do on a regular basis. Though anything daring or dangerous will do, scratch Bonnie and Clyde adventures. Go instead for legal highs, such as:

- Playing competitive sports

- Running a race

- Dancing up a storm

- Participating in a jam session

- Posting a YouTube video

- Doing stand-up comedy

- Joining a drama group

Discover what activity ignites your engine. Then make it happen! You can do better than simply trying to survive the storm that your procrastination creates.

Ending Exercise

Congratulations Crisis-Makers! You've completed this chapter. Now take a moment to simply relax and breathe easily. There's so much valuable information in each section. Although you can read it all, you can't absorb it all—not right away. So, review the change program and choose 1, 2, or 3 skills that you want to implement this week. Once you've gotten those under your belt, then you can go back for more. This program is designed to be a *reference* for you. Take in what you can use now. Then when you're ready to incorporate more skills, return to the program and see what's next for you.

Keep Your Energy Moving Forward
then
Blow Everyone Away with Your Accomplishments!

CHAPTER 7

THE DEFIER PERSONALITY
...BUT WHY SHOULD I DO IT!

Welcome Defiers!

YOU HAVE MANY ENVIABLE QUALITIES. You're unafraid to question authority. You're self-reliant. You're independent. So what could be wrong? Here's the rub. Keeping yourself *apart* from your team rather than *a part of* your team creates friction and tension. Things aren't going your way? Tell him off, then retreat to your virtual friends. Feel she's clipping your wings? Ignore her, then escape to the World of Warcraft.

When I refer to "team," I'm not speaking about a sports team. I'm speaking about your family and work team. Though many people don't think of a family as a team, it is. Indeed, when a family is termed dysfunctional, it's because they're not pulling together for a common purpose the way a team should. When you're part of a team, it doesn't mean you fall into line, buckle down and do what the leader says (unless it's a military team). There's room for disagreement and for doing your own thing. But it does mean that you understand the respective roles of each team member and don't keep bucking the system just to buck the system.

In this chapter, you'll gain a deeper understanding of your defier personality—how it helps you and how it handicaps you. But first, take a mini-version of the quiz you took earlier. See which of these questions resonate with you.

- Do I become sulky, sarcastic, or annoyed when expected to do a task I dislike?

- Do I work slowly or ineffectively in order to sabotage a chore I resent doing?

- Do I blow off my responsibilities by shrugging my shoulders and claiming I've forgotten to do them?

- Do I take offense when others tell me how I could do things differently?

- When people ask me why I did (or didn't do) something, do I view them as hassling or nagging me?

Active and Passive-Aggressive Defiance

When people envision a defier's stance, they typically imagine a person who is hostile: angry lips barking out refusals, arms crossed militantly at the chest, clenched fists shaking in the air. Some defiers do present that body language. Others, however, present quite contrasting images: smiling mouths voicing agreement, open arms suggesting cooperation, nodding heads communicating agreement. This passive form of defiance is called passive-aggressive.

Passive-aggressives may agree to do a task but make little or no effort to follow through. They say "yup, no problem," but never give a second thought to the commitment they have just made. They may shake on it but don't act on it. Such 'yes' folks delude themselves into believing that they're cooperative team members. Rather than owning up to their defiance, they cast themselves as innocent victims stuck in demanding jobs or hard to please relationships—remaining blissfully unaware of how their passive-aggressive stance rouses negative vibes in others.

Both types of defiers (active and passive) relish their independence. Indeed, they may pride themselves on being rebels, mavericks, or a lone voice in the wilderness. Cherishing their autonomy, they're inclined to consider demands on their time as unfair or unjust. Hence, their response to an obligation is often a variation of the defier's signature complaint: *But why should I do it?"* At times, they're questioning the importance of the task at hand: *"...But why **should** I do it?"* Other times, they're implying that the task is an unfair imposition on them: *"...But why should **I** do it?"*

> "It is our attitude at the beginning
> of a difficult task which, more
> than anything else, will affect
> its successful outcome."
> ~ **William James**

In order to more fully understand the defier dynamic, let's now look at the stories of two types of defiers.

Jared and Britney

There's no question that Jared, a salesman for an IT company, is an *actively aggressive defier*. He prides himself on being a fiercely independent person who doesn't need or want anyone to tell him what to do. His verbal outbursts explode with fighting words:

- "She has no f...... idea what she's talking about!"

- "He's tormenting me with that moronic task!"

- "Doesn't that idiot know I have better things to do with my time?"

His defiance is expressed not only in words but also in actions. He has no regrets about petty acts of defiance, like refusing to pay parking tickets or an occasional bout of shop-lifting. Jared admits to having a chip on his shoulder. He sees this as the natural outcome of being raised in a family in which his father's oft repeated lesson to him was: "never, ever let anybody take advantage of you." As he watched his weak mother cave in to his father's demands, it was a no-brainer as to whom he was going to model himself after.

As long as Jared gets to call the shots, relationships progress reasonably well. If others assert their rights, however, his retorts border on the abusive. He interprets friends offering him feedback as controllers who threaten his personal freedom. Though Jared's bummed out about his relationships, he doesn't have the slightest idea about how to improve them. It's so much easier to express righteous indignation, so much more difficult to be introspective.

Now let's turn from Jared, the self-avowed firebrand, to Britney, who exemplifies the subtler *passive-aggressive style*. Britney views herself as a "good person." When asked to do a task, she typically responds, "sure, no problem." But in the course of time, she winds up doing it too slowly, sporadically or halfheartedly to be effective. And on occasion, she simply dodges doing it at all. Lacking introspection, she's baffled by why others are so often annoyed with her.

An example: Britney was 30 minutes late picking up her daughter at the airport. Her excuse: "A friend called, upset about her son doing drugs. I couldn't just hang up on her." When her daughter didn't accept her excuse, Britney was offended. "Why was she so upset? I was helping my friend out. What's the big deal if she waited a few minutes for me?" In this incident, Britney refused to take responsibility for her daughter's distress or her own questionable priorities. All too often, she's like the fabled shoemaker, taking care of others' needs while her own children go shoeless. Though she's not in touch with her defiance, her passive-aggressive behavior frequently creates family dissension.

Despite their differences, both Jared and Britney display the following defier personality traits:

Expressing Defiance by Dawdling

Dawdling offers a non-violent, non-verbal form of protest: a means of exclaiming "No!" indirectly. Though this obviously fits the mold for passive-aggressives, even belligerent defiers are not always openly contentious. At times it's too damaging to act that way. Other times, the opportunity isn't there (the person is not readily available).

Jared, for example, avoids cursing out authority figures to their face. For all his bluster, he's not that self-destructive. Instead, he rages about them to others, expressing his rebellion by refusing to be pinned down to any "artificial deadline" or "stupid rule." Sadly, the only real victim of his rebellion is himself.

Britney, who is more passive than Jared, uses procrastination as her primary form of rebellion. Doing what she wants to do in the moment (rather than what she said she'd do) gives her the sensation that she's taking a bona fide action to assert her individuality. Too bad she doesn't take into account the effect that her breaking her word has on others.

Viewing their Problems as Emanating from the Outside

Defiers are on the lookout for an adversary. After all, you need one if you're looking for a dispute. When those in authority tell them what to do, they impulsively become incensed, interpreting such "orders" as a threat to their individuality. What they fail to appreciate is if they were more grounded in their own agenda, they'd feel less threatened by another's agenda.

Defiers don't stop to consider that tasks that appear to be "unfairly" imposed upon them are often chores they need to do for their own well-being. If they didn't have such a chip on their shoulders, they might even enjoy tackling tasks that they perceive as being "shoved down their throats." We see this characteristic in the ways both Jared and Britney rebel against others' expectations, yet don't identify their own.

Jared, for example, is his own worst enemy when it comes to achieving satisfaction in a job or relationship. By withholding full cooperation with one boss after another, one lover after another, he's only hurting himself. He's like a small child battling his parents' suggestions for self-management because he doesn't want to do what they want him to do. His cavalier attitude toward paying parking tickets is a minor act of insurgency; his occasional bouts of shoplifting are a major and potentially disastrous act of insurgency.

Britney doesn't want to feel that she has to put any boundaries on her moment-by-moment freedom to do what she wants. She doesn't realize that she's thereby making herself a slave to her impulses. Nor does she realize how much she's jeopardizing the relationships that are nearest and dearest to her heart.

Resisting Self-reflection

Defiers are quick to read offenses into the motives and behaviors of others, slow to recognize how their own behavior contributes to their problems. Blaming others is easier than taking stock of themselves. Pointing the finger at another seems particularly justified (in their eyes) when others nag, scold or find fault with them. Too bad they don't acknowledge that if they were on top of their game, there'd be little need for anyone to be badgering them. Typically, they lack clarity about their own goals, complaining that. "If you just left me alone and let me do my own thing, I'd be fine." Ironically, they're the ones who have difficulty defining their "own thing." And they're the ones who view others as adversaries rather than as allies who could assist them in reaching their goals.

When called on their dawdling, defiers reflexively block out the criticism by criticizing the criticizer. Jared, the active defier, drives off his friends when they dare to cross him. When he loses a job, he views it as the inevitable fate of one who is a "true individual, not a phony conformer." In a similar fashion, Britney views herself as the perpetually misconstrued person who is at the mercy of scolds. She's mystified as to why she's so often "unappreciated." It simply isn't her style to question her own role in an interactional dispute.

Hiding Defiance under the Guise of Compliance

This pattern is most apparent in the case of passive-aggressive defiers. We see it in the way Britney responds to interpersonal conflicts. She can't bring herself to openly discuss a disagreement. Instead, she simply repeats her point until (she hopes) the other person sees it her way.

Projecting a positive front while harboring negative thoughts can also be a trait of predominantly active defiers. Face-to-face with his customers, Jared creates an impression of being more agreeable and compliant than he truly is. Later, to "get even" for feeling forced to put on this act, he's slow to provide the agreed-upon service. If Jared would be more honest about his intentions and obligations, he'd become a more honorable, effective salesperson.

Now that we've reviewed the traits that all defiers have in common, let's look at the experience of a small business owner who has occasional bouts of active defiance accompanied by frequent bouts of passive defiance.

Brad: A Defier Personality

Brad's defier tendencies were obvious from the moment he entered my office. "Frankly, I'm here because my wife's been pestering me to come," he announced, "but I doubt that you can do anything for me." It took awhile for Brad to open up, but soon enough he admitted that he was currently going through two crises of his own making.

The Internal Revenue Service was charging him with tax evasion for not filing returns for three years. And he was being forced to pay the total cost of a recent surgical operation because he'd let his health insurance lapse.

Both hassles were a direct result of Brad's ongoing tendency to procrastinate. Yet he skirted around the issue by admitting that though he was "technically at fault" for the two crises, it happened because they were examples of "big institutions trying to squeeze the little guy." Brad's wife, Suzanne, had reached her limit of tolerance for his slacking off and his misplaced accusations. The double whammy of the IRS liability and the lapsed insurance was threatening not only their financial security but also their marriage. The trust and respect she used to have for her husband had swiftly eroded.

Despite Brad's defiant tendencies, he essentially viewed himself as a "nice guy." It helps us to understand his pattern, if we know something about his family background. Brad was raised as a latch-key kid by a single mom. When he was young, she imposed on him a rigorous schedule for homework and household chores. Though he felt she was being unreasonable, he decided it was preferable for him to do things her way than to incur her disfavor.

Though openly a compliant child, Brad had nursed a defiance that ripened as he approached adolescence. Brad viewed it as his "silent rebellion." He'd agree to whatever his mom wanted, then do whatever he pleased. This pattern put him in the power seat. No matter how angry his mother would be about his failure to live up to his word, there was nothing much she could do about it. Her tirades had lost their power to intimidate him.

Wanting to avoid arguing with his mom but longing to get her off his back, Brad became skilled in these passive-aggressive strategies:

- "I'll get to it in a minute, Ma." (never giving it a second thought)

- "I did my homework." (he only did his math homework)

- "Don't worry. I'll clean up my room." (never specifying when)

- "Yeah, I'll do it." (he yells, as he scoots out of the house)

- "I'm doing my homework now." (in 3 minutes, he's back to his baseball cards)

- "That project isn't due till next week." (waiting for the last minute to tend to his responsibilities)

- "As soon as I finish these other things." (always a reason why he can't do it *now*.)

Such childhood passive-aggressive responses are still active in Brad's life today. He refuses to be pinned down to deadlines, doesn't negotiate a compromise and won't directly say 'no'. Instead, his way of "working it out" with others is to agree, then do it his way or simply not do it at all.

Brad's wife says she can't trust anything he says because he's always got a "slippery escape clause," like

- "I forgot."

- "I didn't say I'd do it; I only said I might."

- "I didn't have the time."

- "Quit telling me what to do!"

When Suzanne calls Brad on his excuses, he turns the table on her, by saying: "Aw, come on! Why make such a big deal over this," implying that it's her fault for being upset about such a trivial matter. Suzanne shakes her head in disbelief, concluding that Brad just doesn't "get it."

Procrastinating on the Job

Brad is the owner of a small office supply business. The work itself is not that rewarding, but being his own boss is. "I can't work for someone else," he said. "My last employer was the worst. Anything he told me to do, I wouldn't want to do. Anything he told me not to do, I'd be eager to do."

As it turned out, becoming a boss was not as much fun or as liberating as Brad had imagined. Rather than accepting that every job has its onerous tasks, he found every reason he could to blame the economy, the industry, his employees, and his customers for his difficulties. He admitted that at times he gets so angry, he loses his focus. Once that happens, tasks are only done at the last minute or not done at all.

Brad was not aware that when he was his own boss, he'd need to deal with so many rules, regulations and schedules. As far as he was concerned, being your own boss should mean running things the way you want to. Too bad, he wasn't cognizant of all the governmental regulations and employee issues he'd need to deal with.

Brad now recognizes that he has to make some changes. "This me-against-the-world attitude used to be so satisfying," he confided. "Lately, however, it hasn't had that effect. In fact, it causes me tremendous stress. My stomach is in knots, I don't sleep well, and I look like hell."

Procrastinating at Home

By the time Brad came to see me, his personal life was in shambles. Unable to explain, cajole, argue, or browbeat him into changing his ways, his wife was on the verge of leaving him. And the IRS suit and a huge medical bill were impossible to ignore. Nevertheless, his response to these matters was to cling tenaciously to the defiant position that had gotten him into so much trouble in the first place. Whether he was talking to me about his marriage, his finances, his work relationship or his household routines, he'd utter the same phrase over and over again: "I'll be damned if I'm going to let people push me around!"

Here's how Brad described the state of his marriage. "My wife gets ticked off about some trivial thing I've forgotten to do and keeps bitching about it: 'You never do what you say you'll do.' In response to her craziness, I laugh. I don't know why. I guess to lighten her up. When she keeps harping on me, I dig my heels in even more. I want her to see how stupid she is to be bothered by such small stuff."

Brad prefers to settle such marital disputes with a laugh, a kiss, a joke—whatever—anything but an in-depth discourse that might require compromise, concession or conciliation. And so he baits her, negates her, turns a deaf ear to her. Of course, that only makes her angrier. "I know my way is not always the best way," he admits, "but it does make me feel like I'm top dog. Sometimes that's the only way I can express any power in this relationship."

Brad's First Steps: Beginning the Change Program:

Brad kicked off his change program by developing constructive responses to his wife's complaints rather than responding with knee-jerk defiance. To implement this change, Brad had to have a few simple responses in his back pocket that he could utilize whenever needed. He settled on: "ok," "good idea," "I'll think about it," "I'll get back to you on that." As we worked together, Brad adopted other easy-to-learn techniques to tone down his rebellious nature. You can learn them, too. Here's how:

THE DEFIER'S CHANGE PROGRAM
Beat Your Procrastination Habit *and* Be Your Own Person

If you scored high on the defier quiz, you probably noticed an abundance of similarities between Brad's procrastination patterns and your own. But you're not Brad. You've got your own history and style of living. Now it's time for you to pull the curtain aside and take a closer look at your story. Doing so will enable you to gain a deeper understanding of your own issues. So, take a few moments to do a self-assessment exercise. Be one of the 20% of readers who will *do* the exercise, not just skim through it. Remember, the program works if you work the program.

> "Tell me I'll forget, show me,
> I may remember, but involve
> me and I'll understand."
> **~ Chinese Proverb**

1. Recall an occasion when you were faced with a task that you were expected to do but didn't do—as an act of defiance. Reflecting on that occasion, ask yourself these questions:

    • Whom or what were you defying?

    • What consequences occurred because you didn't do the task?

    • Do you reflect on this occasion now as a missed opportunity? If yes, why?

2. Recall an occasion when you said you'd do a task but didn't honor your commitment. Reflecting on that occasion, ask yourself these questions:

    • What stirred up your passive-aggressive resistance?

    • Thinking about it now, do you believe it was a worthy act of defiance?

    • Does your passive-aggressive tendency have a negative effect on your career, relationships, self-esteem?

Congratulations. If you took the time to do the above exercise, you've shown that you're serious about understanding the dynamics of your procrastination. Armed with this understanding, you'll be in a better position to modify your patterns—retaining what works for you, toning down what doesn't. Now, let's delve into specific strategies to help you beat your procrastination pattern.

Guided Imagery for Your Creative Mind

How do you think your life would be different if you used your energy to work toward your goals rather than to resist the status quo? Not sure? Perhaps the following guided imagery will help you gain a clearer picture.

To begin, read the visualization slowly until you feel comfortable with its content. Then, either let someone else read you the instructions with a slow, relaxed voice or record these guidelines for your personal use which you can then replay whenever you wish. As you record the guided imagery, be sure to speak in a slow, soothing voice. Pause for thirty seconds between each instruction.

Assume a comfortable position in a place that is quiet, dimly lit, and free from distractions. Some people prefer lying down with their legs straight and slightly apart, their arms extended loosely at their side. Others prefer to sit in a relaxed mode in a comfortable chair, couch or bed.

Close your eyes and take a few deep breaths to clear your mind and relax your body inhaling *s-l-o-w-l-y* through your nose, exhaling *s-l-o-w-l-y* through your mouth. Let go of any tension or tightness in your body. Allow the thoughts and cares of the day to drift away, leaving your body light, your mind empty.

Beginning with your present age, *slowly count backwards five years at a time,* pausing at each age to develop images of what your life was like for you when you were younger. Stop when you reach the last age for which you have clear memories (for most people, that's between the ages of four and seven).

Remaining at this last age, imagine yourself *engaged in a pleasurable activity* that you used to do when you were much younger (i.e. playing ball, running, singing, dancing, painting, building). As you see yourself involved in this activity, notice how your body feels. Picture the expression on your face. Allow yourself to feel pleasure in simply enjoying the pursuit.

Gradually bring this play to a close. Then return to your present age. Picture a specific task in your present life that you don't want to do, but that you realize needs to be done. Imagine (even if it's not true) that *you've chosen* to do this undertaking using your own free will. Then go about doing it in the same playful way that you went about doing the childhood activity.

Visualize yourself completing this task and feeling good about what you've done. Take pride in the fact that you chose to work on this project without resentment or resistance. Stay with the pleasant emotions you're feeling.

Now, hear a voice inside you saying, "You can enjoy doing a task even if *someone else tells you to do it*. Being enthusiastic about an activity helps you feel energized and empowered." Pause for a moment to realize the truth in these words.

Take as much time as you need and whenever you're ready, slowly open your eyes. Take time to absorb the meaning of your visualization before you move on to the next section.

Enhancing Your Thinking Skills

View what Others Want as a Request, not a Demand.

Though you're not always the quarterback calling the plays, you are a member of a team (your family, work group, community, country). And it's often in your best interests to cooperate with your team to get the mission accomplished. Yes, this may mean taking the garbage out when you don't feel like it or paying your taxes on time or completing petty paper work. Does this mean that you can't negotiate or compromise with other team members? Or suggest alternative ways to do a task? Of course not. But you won't be able to do any of those things, if you're so wrapped up in your defiance.

Hence, instead of rousing yourself into rebellion when you're expected to do a task, think more temperately. Become empowered by deciding *how* you will respond. Are you going to choose to look for another job and/or speak up and attempt to create some changes in the workplace? Are you going to take responsibility for taking the garbage out or negotiate the household chores with your partner? Recognize where your power lies instead of resisting power that's not yours.

Reflect on Alternative Ways to Respond—other than Defiance.

Identify signs that you may be reacting defiantly. For example, when someone asks you to do a task, does your mind race with reasons as to why you shouldn't have to do it? Do you curse out the task? Or berate the person who gave it to you? Do you think it's so unfair? Do you spend more time thinking about how to get out of a chore than simply taking the time to do it?

Tone down your oppositional reaction. Be creative not rigid. Think about alternative responses that are not pie-in-the-sky options (i.e. instead of handing in a weekly task report, suggest a monthly one). Alternatives that are more reasonable are more likely to be acceptable to others (i.e. I'll pick up our son at day care after work, if you drop him off in the morning).

Generate Multiple Options for How to Respond to a Situation.

As you generate multiple responses, make sure your responses satisfy some of the other person's expectations as well as some of your own (a win-win situation). Let's suppose, for example, that you've been assigned an especially difficult field research project to do at work. Without giving it much thought, you'd probably choose one of these options:

- **Comply**—Say nothing and begin the project even though your heart isn't in it.

- **Defy**—Balk at doing it, allowing your resentment to fester, your procrastination to flourish.

- **Passive-Aggressive**—Agree to do it but use delay tactics that undermine your action.

Whichever one of these options you choose, chances are you won't do well and won't enjoy the task. Imagine how much more productive you'd be if you applied constructive, creative thought to what you could do instead of being reflexively compliant or defiant. Here are just a few options you might consider:

- *Discuss* possible strategies for the project with your supervisor so that the project itself doesn't seem so intimidating. A bonus: You may improve your relationship with him, if you present your ideas in a well thought-out manner.

- *Divide* the project into separate, smaller tasks. Then, figure out how you might go about getting each individual portion of the task accomplished most efficiently.

- *Map out* ways to shift competing responsibilities to alternate time frames in order to make more time for this project. (No, you can't do it all!)

- *Negotiate* with your supervisor to discover what flexibility she might have in any of her expectations.

• *Figure out* alternative ways to approach the project. Others will be more open to hearing you—if they believe that you're not just trying to get out of the work. When presenting your options, be specific and positive. Veer away from being global and negative.

Choose Your Battles Carefully, Weighing what's Worth Fighting for.

Reserve your acts of rebellion for important issues. Maybe there's a situation in which you truly are being taken advantage of. Or a rule that's clearly discriminatory. Or an environmental issue that's offensive to your morality. For these types of situations, be a rebel!

> "Never doubt that a small group of thoughtful, committed citizens can change the world; indeed, it's the only thing that ever has."
>
> ~ Margaret Mead

But don't be a rebel without a cause. Though you may think of yourself as a trailblazer, make sure you're not fooling yourself. Many a narcissist masquerades as a rebel, their dissent based on nothing deeper than: 'I don't want to do what I don't want to do.'

Cultivate an Internal Nurturing Parent.

Our personalities are made up of many diverse components. As a defier, I'm sure you're aware of your critical part—critical not only toward others but also toward yourself. But what do you know about your nurturing part? Not sure? Well then, do the following exercise.

To-Do Exercise

Take a slow, deep breath. Relax. Now imagine that inside of you there lives a nurturing parent who is your very best friend. This parent is *not* harsh, critical, or quick to berate you for what you haven't done. Neither is he or she a sidekick whom you use to support your own worst impulses. Rather, this nurturing parent is a mentor who speaks with maturity, compassion and wisdom, motivating you to attend to what you need to do—even when you don't want to do it. When you're tempted to blow off your responsibilities, ask your inner nurturing parent questions such as:

- *Why* should I do this work when I don't want to?

- *What* would be a compelling way to tackle this project?

- *When* would be a good time to begin the work?

Then answer the questions you pose. Your inner parent, like any nurturing parent, will remind you of basic truths that you might otherwise overlook.

- Not everything you do has to feel good in the moment.

- Short-term defiance often leads to long-term regrets.

- What you delay doing today is often harder to do tomorrow.

Enriching Your Speaking Skills

Mean What You Say; Say What You Mean.

Advice for passive-aggressives: don't say what others want to hear just to appease them. Don't commit to doing a task if you don't intend to do it. If you do commit and then change your mind, take responsibility for the change and tell the person involved.

For example, you might say, "I know I told you I'd take care of it this week, but I was feeling lethargic and didn't get to it." You can then propose a revised deadline. "I've fallen behind in our group project. How about changing our meeting time to Wednesday after I get a chance to catch up?"

> *"People change and forget*
> *to tell one another."*
> ~ Lillian Hellman

Be Slower to Use Confrontational Talk.

Minimize your use of confrontational discourse, such as:

- "You gave me an unfair review!"

- "You're always on my case!"

- "You expect too much from me!"

Notice what the above complaints have in common. They're all negative gripes and they all begin with "you." Though speaking this way may provide you with a chance to let off steam, it doesn't help resolve the conflict. To be more effective, begin your sentences with "I."

- "I believe I deserve a better review; here's why…"

- "I was late because the job was more complex than I expected."

- "I appreciate receiving recognition for the work I do."

Do you hear the difference in tone? Are you aware that the second set of statements are less blaming, less complaining, less attacking and more open to exploring a solution to the problem?

> *"Maturity begins when we're content to feel we're right about something without feeling the necessity to prove someone else wrong."*
> ~ **Sydney Harris**

Limit Your Whining.

Health experts say that one or two glasses of wine a day is good for your health; anything more than that should be avoided. My take on it:

> One or two *whines* a day is good for your health; anything more than that should be avoided.

A little whining may actually improve your outlook on obligations. After all, life can be difficult. When things don't go your way, you have to find some way to let off steam.

- "It's not fair!"

- "She shouldn't have said that."

- "That's just not right."

You complain, you grumble, you tell your story to one or two empathetic friends. Presto, you feel better. Astonishingly simple and effective therapy!

But whining that goes on day after day, well, that's a whine of another sort. Virtuoso whiners typically perfect their art in childhood. Since whining is so grating on the nerves, kids learn that it's an effective way to manipulate parents. Weakened by so much whining, Mom and Dad may give in to the most outrageous demands just to gain some peace and quiet. Like other childhood traits, however, whining is an activity that's best outgrown as people mature.

To be a winner, limit your whining. When you've reached your two whines a day, you may be stymied as to what to do if you're still feeling frustrated. Here are a few suggestions:

- When problems arise, search for solutions.

- When disappointments occur, accept them.

- When others annoy you, shrug it off.

- When a situation needs to be addressed, speak up.

Perhaps the worst outcome of persistent whining is that once it becomes habitual, that's the trait that people will remember about you.

> *"People will forget what you said, people will forget what you did, but people will never forget how you made them feel."*
> **~ Maya Angelou**

Apologize if You haven't Done what You Said You would Do.

Some people hate making apologies, equating it with an admission of failure or incompetence.

- "I'm such a screw-up!"

- "I messed up again."

- "I never do anything right!"

No need to go from one extreme (no apology) to the opposite extreme (self-flagellation). Simply express your regrets. An apology is a courtesy, a way to show that what you did (or didn't do) adversely affected the other person. It can also be a prelude toward renegotiating a better future, as in "Sorry I didn't return your call sooner; let's set a time now to get together."

One more essential point about apologies: Avoid getting into too many situations where an apology is called for. Empty apologies are worse than none, as people will learn not to take your apology seriously. Indeed, offering an apology without doing better next time is a hallmark of passive-aggressive behavior.

To-Do Exercise

Write down at least three types of authentic apologies. Make sure they're honest and appropriate. Don't denigrate your own character or you'll hesitate to use them. Here are my three favorites:

- Sorry (simple but honest)

- I regret not taking care of…

- I feel bad that I didn't…

If you like mine, take them. Own them. Use them. Put your own spin on them. Or create your own.

Avoid Speaking in a Non-stop, Negative Soliloquy.

Here are two descriptive sentences. Which one do you think is more likely to trigger your tendency to procrastinate?

- "It's a tough undertaking with tons of work required."

- "It's a tough undertaking with tons of work required but I'm learning a lot."

The first sentence is so negative, why even bother to do the work? Seems like a hopeless cause. The second sentence balances out the picture. Yes, you don't like all the effort required, yet you appreciate that you're learning something important from the process. Reminding yourself about both the positive and negative aspects of a task can be a big motivator, especially when your first impulse is to put the task off.

Be Aware of Your Non-verbal Communication.

Accepting responsibility for not only *what* you say but *how* you say it is an essential step toward creating constructive communication. Tape your voice. Does your voice sound hostile, hesitant, challenging, condescending, mean-spirited or sarcastic?

Linguistic studies reveal that at least 80% of communication is conveyed by tone of voice, body language, facial expression and non-verbal gestures. Words said in a snide tone convey an entirely different meaning than if they're communicated in a sincere tone. To avoid misunderstandings and unproductive confrontations, match your voice to your words. If you say "yes" with your words but "no" with your voice, don't be surprised if people don't buy what you're selling.

Expanding Your Action Skills

Strive to Act, not React

Acting is making a choice—not defiantly, not compliantly—but because you've given thought to the situation and made your decision. Reacting is responding reflexively to another's actions or words.

Acting is empowering, whether you get what you want or you don't. For example, if you believe it will be difficult for you to complete a writing project by its due date, you may choose to ask your editor if you can have more time, explaining why.

- If the response is "yes," you've gotten what you want. (Just be sure you don't blow the new deadline.)

- If the answer is a "yes but...," you can then decide how you want to deal with what comes after the "but."

- If the answer is "no," you're no worse off than you were initially.

You don't always get what you want just because you advocate on your own behalf. Yet, you can still feel pleased with yourself that you've acted in an empowering manner.

To solidify this example, reflect on the difference between the role of a powerful adult and a powerless child. Adults, at least those who behave like adults, *act* by figuring out when and how to take care of their obligations. Children, at least those who aren't 4 going on 40, *react* by whining, wailing, pleading or throwing a temper tantrum when they don't get what they want. All unseemly behaviors—particularly when you're no longer a kid.

Take Responsibility for Doing what Needs to be Done.

Take charge of your own responsibilities. Don't wait until you fall behind, creating a need for a parental figure to berate, punish or nag you about your obligations. If you need a reminder (and who doesn't), use technology. Gadgets can beep you, buzz you, and gently remind you about what you need to attend to. If you're the non-tech type, use a kitchen timer, a calendar, or a Post-it note taped to a place you have to see (your bathroom mirror, refrigerator door or coffee cup).

Which would you prefer to do?

Figure out a way to remind yourself what you need to do?

or

Have someone else berate you for what you didn't do?

Work *with* Your Team, not *against* it.

As independent as you'd like to imagine you are, you're still dependent upon others. Perhaps you're dependent on a family member for running a smooth household, friends for your emotional well-being, your supervisor for your work review. This doesn't make you a weak person; it's just a dose of reality.

Whether you're on the job with your co-workers, at a social event with friends or at home with family, things go a lot smoother when you function as a team player. Hence, get into the habit of supporting and aiding. Give up the habit of withholding and obstructing. Be open to accommodating what the team needs as well as what you, as an individual, need.

Polish up Your Assertiveness and Conflict Resolution Skills.

It may seem counterproductive to become more assertive if you're already a defier. Isn't that for passive people who can't speak up for themselves? Yes and no. When I used to teach assertiveness training courses for adults, many of my students were indeed passive people who needed to gain the skills, strategies and confidence to become more assertive. Other students, however, were aggressive people. They were there because loved ones had paid for them to attend, hoping they would learn how to sandpaper down their rough edges. Though these students thought they were being appropriately assertive, they needed to know that others experienced them as aggressive, abrasive and even abusive.

Assertiveness training as well as conflict resolution programs can teach you to become more empowered by:

- Initiating ideas

- Eliciting information

- Expressing concerns

- Clarifying misunderstandings

- Forging compromises

- Proposing changes

- Motivating others—and more

Becoming proficient in the above skills will have a huge pay-off—both in your personal and work relationships.

To-Do Exercise

Imagine that you're the lucky recipient of a gift certificate to an assertiveness training course. Although your first impulse is to toss the certificate in the garbage, you give it a second thought. Now that you're no longer letting defiance define your behavior, write down three valuable skills you might learn in such a course. Then, go to your favorite search engine to find articles on those topics. Pick out your favorites. Cut and paste excerpts from them into a file. Review them each week for a month.

Having trouble coming up with a topic? Here are three suggestions:

- How to resolve conflict

- How to communicate well with authority figures

- How to tame your anger

While you're on the Internet, take the time to check out a few archived columns on my web site *www.PsychWisdom.com*. Three articles that might be helpful to you are:

- How to Respond to a Put-Down

- The Passive-Aggressive Personality

- Young, Bored and Floundering

Get Involved in Pursuits where You can Do Things *Your* Way.

As you gain control of *some* aspects of your life, you'll have less need to control *all* aspects of your life. Hence, use your energy to be innovative, not defiant. Develop creative, constructive projects that you can completely control, such as:

- Creative activity: i.e. writing a song, painting a picture

- Athletic activity: i.e. running a marathon, shooting hoops

- Organizational activity: i.e. organizing your music, your photos

Ending Exercise

Congratulations Defiers! You've completed this chapter. Now take a moment to simply relax and breathe easily. There's so much valuable information in each section. Although you can read it all, you can't absorb it all—not right away. So, review the change program and choose 1, 2, or 3 skills that you want to implement this week. Once you've gotten those under your belt, then go back for more. This program is designed to be *a reference* for you. Take in what you can use now. Then when you're ready to incorporate more skills, return to the program and see what's next for you.

Honor Your Commitments
then
Rejoice in Your Success!

CHAPTER 8

THE PLEASER PERSONALITY
...BUT I CAN'T SAY "NO!"

Welcome Pleasers!

YOU HAVE MANY LAUDABLE QUALITIES. You're a people person. You're good-natured. You're helpful to others. So what could be wrong? Here's the rub. Pleasers find it easy to say "yes" to what others want. Sounds good. However, with so much on your plate, *your* needs end up at the bottom of the pile. The dizzying array of tasks you face is not because you're a workaholic but because you have trouble saying "no." Time for you to chill out before you burn out!

In this chapter, you'll gain a deeper understanding of your pleaser personality—how it helps you and how it handicaps you. But first, take a mini-version of the quiz you took earlier. See which of these questions resonate with you.

- Do I have difficulty saying "no" to people who ask for help, yet feel resentful later on?

- Do I get over-involved with other people's problems, postponing attention to my own?

- Do I run around doing a million things, yet often feel that I haven't accomplished much?

- Do I have a strong need for approval from others?

- Do I often complain that "I have no time," "I've too much to do," "I'm sooo busy?"

It's so easy to feel frazzled and fried in our speed-oriented culture. Work harder! Finish it faster! Make it better! Though this is troubling for many, it's particularly troubling for pleasers. Why? Because pleasers care what others think. Add on the abundance of responsibilities that they've assumed and life can easily spin out of control. You know what I'm talking about, right?

In your saner moments, you do know that you can't do everything—even though some media stories try to convince you otherwise. Attempt to do too much and you'll be operating on overload. To truly understand what that means, let's check out what occurs when an electrical circuit is overloaded.

It's almost dinner time. You're working hard trying to get a report done and sit down to a decent meal (you're tired of eating unhealthy, fattening food). All of a sudden, you find yourself in total darkness. The circuit breaker has popped. Nothing is working. No lights, no computer, no printer, no scanner, no microwave, no chargers, no toaster, no air-conditioning, no TV, no land phone, no nothing. What do you do?

You rush to the electrical panel with your non-tech flashlight to search for the popped breaker. You flip the breaker back on and return to doing your stuff. Just as you've settled in, pop, you're in total darkness again. Bummer! You realize you forgot to turn off a few electrical doodads before you returned to work. What a pain this circuit breaker is. Then you remember what a circuit breaker is designed to do. It's *a safety device*, protecting you from fire that would undoubtedly occur if you continued to operate on overload.

You recognize that you, too, are operating on overload, with your harried, pressured, stressed life. If you didn't have so much to do, you wouldn't be so stressed about putting dinner on the table. If you weren't so stressed about putting dinner on the table, you wouldn't be so nervous about your upcoming evaluation at work. If you weren't so nervous about that evaluation, you wouldn't be so annoyed with your kid's thoughtless quip. If you weren't so upset with your kid's thoughtless quip, you wouldn't have this pounding headache. Get the picture?

Too bad that you don't have circuit breakers built into your system to alert you of impending overload. Or, do you? Yes you do!

- *Chronic stress* is a way your body is telling you, "Stop! You're damaging me. Treat me better or I won't function well!"

- *Chronic angst* is a way your mind is telling you, "Chill out! You can't live this way. Give me a break!"

- *Chronic disappointment* is a way your relationships are telling you, "Slow down! You need time to just enjoy each other."

Ignore warning signals that are designed to protect you from harm and you can do serious damage to your mind, body and relationships. I hope you're wise enough not to let that happen. To gain a better understanding of the pleaser personality, let's now take a look at Maria and Ted's stories.

Maria and Ted

We'll begin with Maria, a graduate student, who illustrates the social pleaser type. Maria admits to being an approval junkie, judging her worth on how popular she is. Since Maria's social life takes precedence, it's no surprise that her academic life suffers the consequences. Though she doesn't view herself as a procrastinator, Maria does acknowledge that she never seems to have time to complete her doctoral thesis. She thinks her problem is that she has no discipline, no loyalty to personal priorities. Not only doesn't she give her thesis priority, she's also vague about her long-term goals. "I'm not sure what I'll do when I complete my doctorate, so I figure there's no rush in getting it."

Maria keeps so busy with her social life—hanging with friends, responding to a barrage of text messages, writing a blog, and, of course, partying that her doctoral dissertation inadvertently ends up at the bottom of her priority list. "I need to keep busy," she admitted, "because when I don't, I feel empty. My dissertation is lonely work and makes me feel so alone. To counteract that, I connect with my Twitter and Facebook friends and before I know it, the afternoon is gone."

> *"The worst loneliness is not to be comfortable with yourself."*
> ~ **Mark Twain**

Ted, a fifty-two-year-old physician, has succeeded in realizing all of his major life goals. He has a thriving general practice, a beautiful wife, three great kids, and a showcase home. His tendency toward pleasing others, however, is turning his dream life into a nightmare.

Ted acknowledges that he chose to become a family physician so that he could treat the whole patient, not just a symptom. Yet his working style coupled with recent changes in health care make his original goal a distant memory. He now schedules patients every 10 minutes—barely giving himself enough time to say more than "hello," then wonders why he's always feeling rushed.

Ted takes pride in being able to account for and justify every minute of his time. If he's not seeing patients, he's running to the hospital, teaching a course, reading a journal or attending a conference. His rushed use of time is at the expense of his desire to be there for others. His patients are agitated with his waiting time, his wife is upset that he's never home, his kids view him as an adjunct member of the family, and his friends have fallen by the wayside.

Ted's pattern of taking on responsibility began early in life. "I've always been the strong one in my family," he stated. "My father died when I was fifteen. This instantly made me 'the man of the house.' I started working then to bring in extra money for the family. That's when I developed a habit of being busy all the time. It seemed to be the responsible thing to do. Yet, I'm always feeling hassled."

Though Ted says he thrives on multi-tasking, he neglects to notice its cost. His family complains that they can never have a conversation with him without his being distracted by something else. Though he has his moments of regret, he doesn't see what he can do about it. So, he carries on the only way he knows how: by trying to please everyone and, in the process, pleasing no one.

We've seen several significant contrasts between the portraits of Maria and Ted. Still they have much in common. Here are the characteristics that pleasers share:

Feeling Uncomfortable Saying "No"

Pleasers believe that saying "no" is being selfish. Actually, it may be far more self-serving to say "yes," just to earn approval from others or from an erroneous belief that you have no choice.

> *"I don't know the key to success but the key to failure is to try to please everyone."*
> ~ **Bill Cosby**

Both Maria and Ted reflexively say "yes," regardless of whether they have the time, energy or desire to make another commitment. This definitely takes its toll on their primary goals. Maria is too socially oriented to focus on her educational goals, while Ted is too keen on keeping busy all the time to notice how it's impacting his significant relationships.

Basing Your Value on Others' Approval

Pleasers can't shake the notion that their value and self-worth are dependent on how others perceive them. Though they may present as self-confident, their inner feelings rarely match their outer demeanor. Being constantly busy is one way for them to prove their worthiness, yet strangely enough, they never quite believe that they're doing enough.

This trait manifests itself in the way Maria give excess importance to her social life, becoming bored or bewildered when she's alone. And in the way Ted feels that no matter how much he's achieved in life, it's still never enough.

> "What we must decide is how we are valuable—rather than how valuable we are."
> ~ Edgar Friedenberg

Lacking Self-discipline for Personal Goals

Instead of actively making a decision as to *what* they're going to do and *when* and *how* they're going to do it, pleasers passively let their time drift to whatever or whoever is calling for them in the moment. By keeping themselves so continuously busy, they don't take the time to create a viable, sustainable work schedule.

Unfortunately, the easiest tasks to put off without disturbing others are personal needs and goals. And so Maria, for example, does not take the time she needs to complete her doctoral dissertation or reflect on her future career goals; while Ted lets his personal relationships fall by the wayside, as he involves himself in work related activities from morning to evening.

Difficulty Creating and Maintaining Priorities

Pleasers have trouble deciding what tasks should take top priority. As hard as it is to prioritize projects within one field of endeavor (i.e. determining what work tasks to accomplish on any particular day), it becomes even harder to establish priorities among tasks in different fields (i.e. determining the relative importance of social, personal, health, career, and relationship responsibilities).

Maria, for instance, stays heavily involved with her virtual friends to the detriment of her dissertation. Clearly something has to give if she's not going to end up being an ABD (all but dissertation). Though Ted likes being busy on all fronts, the quality of his life suffers because of it. Like Maria, he confuses "more" with "better."

Creating a Balanced Life

Pleasers are most familiar with two polarized states of being: being overly busy or being buggy when they're not. Often pleasers say they wish they could just relax. Yet when the opportunity presents itself, they're somehow at a loss. A well-balanced life forever eludes them.

Maria, for instance, doesn't enjoy whatever downtime she has. She feels empty when alone. Her value, she believes, is in being with others. Ted feels similarly barren inside. He admits, "I grew up too fast. I wish I could be a kid again without a care in the world."

Now that we've reviewed the traits that pleasers have in common, let's get more closely acquainted with Diana, an office manager and self-described "workaholic."

Diana: A Pleaser Personality

Diana initially sought out my services because of a growing sadness. The immediate cause was the recent death of her friend who passed away after a prolonged bout with cancer. This event was certainly upsetting enough on its own, but it also served as a prompt to get Diana to reassess her life. And she disliked what she saw. "I'm pushing myself to be Superwoman and it's taking its toll," Diana told me at our first meeting. "My friend's death made me realize how off target my life is. I've got to focus on what's important instead of trying to do everything."

Diana attributed her Superwoman drive to her dread that she might otherwise end up like her mother. "My mom stayed home with us kids and it dried her up inside," Diana explained. "I swore I would never let that happen to me. I wanted to prove that I could do it all—hold down a job, keep my husband happy, be a nurturing mom, keep up with my extended family, be there for friends and more. But now I see that I'm kidding myself. I'm trying to please everyone and I'm ending up pleasing no one—myself included."

Diana was aware that she attempted to do too much. She knew she was feeling emotionally and physically drained. Despite this awareness, however, she couldn't seem to create any meaningful change in her life. In seeking out my coaching services, she was hoping that I could help her modify her pattern.

Procrastinating at Work

Diana, an office manager, readily identified herself as a "workaholic." Yet, she had a serious misperception about what that word meant. Though she correctly interpreted it as "a person who can't stop working," she also perceived it as someone who was a "superior worker." In fact, there are important differences between a superior worker and a workaholic.

The superior worker is one who works *efficiently and effectively*, managing her resources well, creating time for self-renewing activities that keep her mind, body and energy humming. By contrast, the workaholic is one who works *compulsively*, trying to please everyone, leaving little time for self-renewal activities. Because the superior worker knows her priorities and controls her commitments, she typically meets her deadlines. The workaholic, despite working long hours, often misses deadlines as her focus and energy are spread too thin.

Although Diana is indeed a high achiever, she earned that title, in spite of, not because of her workaholic tendencies. As she herself put it, "I work like a crazy woman. Whatever assignment I take on, I do it all—whether it really should be done by me or done at all." To achieve this, she works through lunch time and way past quitting time. As she tries to keep up with it all, not a day goes by in which she doesn't feel muscle spasms, shoulder pains or headaches.

Summing up her job, Diana said, "I feel driven by the demands of the machines—the phone, fax, intercom, e-mail, and above all, the clock. No matter how fast I work, at the end of the day, there's always more to do. It's so frustrating; I can never keep up with it all." Yet Diana thought she had no choice but to keep on doing what she was doing. Office manager that she was, she never addressed the proactive notion of how she might *manage* her responsibilities.

Procrastinating at Home

Diana's description of her home life made it sound as stressful as her work life. "Other people see home as a place to relax. I definitely do not. To me, it's just another place where I work hard. There are always a zillion things to do around the house. And being a mother has come down to being on call to drive my kids someplace or do something for them that they insist is an absolutely necessity. I'm so worn out by the end of the day that I confess—even sex has become a chore."

On those rare occasions when she had free time, she'd spin her mental wheels about tasks still undone. When her husband saw how stressed she was, he suggested she take a day off—just for herself. Diana's immediate response was: "I don't know; I might have to complete some work at home; the kids might need me to do something; I can't make any definite plans." Though Diana viewed her life as out of control, she couldn't see any way to ease the pressure. Her focus was on what *others* might want or need, not on what *she* might want or need. She didn't reflect on her choices; she simply assumed that she must be there to meet the expectations of others.

As we were reminiscing about her teen years, Diana recalled being embarrassed by her outlook on pleasing others. "Whatever I thought would please Jeff, my boyfriend, I would do. And I'm not only talking about sex. I'd go to his house and clean up his room. My friends thought I was nuts, but I figured what's the big deal? I like to organize things, so I'll organize his stuff. I knew he needed it—his room was a mess, stuff all over the place. I didn't see then that I was setting a pattern for my future."

As we continued to work together, Diana became increasingly introspective. The first time I asked her, "What do *you want* to do?" she was stymied by the question. She knew what she *should* do. She knew what *others wanted* her to do. But she had never given much thought to what *she* wanted to do. It was time for Diana to focus on herself.

> *"Your vision will become clear only*
> *when you look into your heart.*
> *Who looks outside, dreams.*
> *Who looks inside, awakens."*
> ~ Carl Jung

Diana's First Steps: Beginning the Change Program:

Diana started her change program by being more aware of her own goals. If she could do that, she reasoned, then she wouldn't be so susceptible to attending to random events of the day or to yielding to other people's priorities.

Before Diana made a new commitment, she deliberately reflected on whether it was *her* agenda or whether it belonged to someone else. To make this skill work, she knew she had to make the word "no" an active part of her vocabulary. But as a pleaser, she needed to be able to say "no" in a pleasing way. *"No, not at this time; but thanks for asking me,"* became one of her pet phrases.

THE PLEASER'S CHANGE PROGRAM
Beat Your Procrastination Habit *and* Be Helpful to Others

If you scored high on the pleaser quiz, you probably noticed an abundance of similarities between Diana's procrastination patterns and your own. But you are not Diana. You've got your own history and style of living. Now it's time for you to pull the curtain aside and take a closer look at your story. Doing so will enable you to gain a deeper understanding of what saps your time and energy. Take a few moments now to do a self-assessment exercise. Be one of the 20% of people who will *do* the exercise, not just skim through it. Remember, the program works if you work the program.

> *"Tell me I'll forget, show me, I may remember, but involve me and I'll understand."*
> **~ Chinese Proverb**

1. Recall an occasion when you neglected to do what you wanted to do because you were distracted by what someone else wanted. Reflecting on that occasion, answer these questions:

   • What specifically kept you from doing what you wanted to do?

   • Looking back on it, do you think that was a good choice?

- What were the consequences of neglecting your own desires? Do you reflect on it now as a missed opportunity? If yes, why?

2. Recall an occasion when you finished a task but got it done late because you did much more than you needed to do in an attempt to please or impress another. Now, answer these questions:

   - Whom were you trying to please?

   - Why was pleasing this person so important to you?

   - Do you regret putting so much time into this task? Why?

Congratulations. If you took the time to answer these questions, you've shown that you're serious about understanding the dynamics of your procrastination. Armed with this understanding, you'll be in a better position to modify your patterns—reinforcing what works for you, toning down what doesn't. Now, let's delve into the change program that's tailor-made for pleasers.

Guided Imagery for Your Creative Mind

When you're saddled with obligations, your need to relax is low or non-existent. What you may fail to recognize, is how essential relaxation is for maintaining good mental and physical health. The following imagery encourages you to rise above daily difficulties and enter into a more peaceful state of being.

To begin, read the visualization slowly until you feel comfortable with its content. Then, either let someone else give you the instructions at a slow, relaxed pace or record these guidelines, for your personal use, which you can then replay whenever you wish. As you record them, be sure to speak in a slow, soothing voice. Pause for thirty seconds between each instruction.

Assume a comfortable position in a place that is quiet, dimly lit, and free from distractions. Some people prefer lying down with their legs straight and slightly apart, their arms extended loosely at their side. Others prefer to sit in a relaxed mode in a comfortable chair, couch or bed.

Close your eyes and take a few deep breaths to clear your mind and relax your body—inhaling s-l-o-w-l-y through your nose, exhaling s-l-o-w-l-y through your mouth. Let go of any tension or tightness in your body. Allow the thoughts and cares of the day to drift away, leaving your body light, your mind empty.

Now, imagine that you're *walking along a path* in a densely wooded area. You don't know where you are but you're content to keep walking until you find a place where you can rest and gain your bearings.

You keep walking along the path which leads deeper into the woods until you reach a fork where the path splits into two. Both paths look the same. You don't know which one to take. Not wanting to waste time, you *proceed down the one to your right*, though you feel uncertain and rushed.

As you continue to walk down this path, you notice that the trees are now closer together. You're a bit worried that you may get lost. You come to another crossroads: one path on your left, another on your right, and a third straight ahead. All three paths look the same, and you don't know which one to take. Not wanting to waste time, you *proceed down the one to the left*, but you still feel uncertain and rushed.

You keep on walking. You turn a bend and there are trees in front of you, but no path. You turn around. You can't see the path anywhere! *You are truly lost among all these trees.* Feel the tension in your body rise as you realize how disoriented you are.

Though you're frightened, you tell yourself to stop and think. Visualize yourself leaning against a tree, breathing slowly as you try to calm down. You gaze into the woods, noticing *a tower directly ahead*. You walk amongst the trees until you reach the tower. At the tower, you see steps leading to the top and you climb them.

Now that you're at the peak of the tower, you can clearly see over the surrounding treetops. Look around and notice that there are many other towers scattered throughout the woods. Directly ahead of you, you see a river with a path running along its near bank. *The path ends at a small inn with a "Welcome" sign out front.* You feel relieved at what you see.

You climb down the tower and walk toward the river. As you approach the river, you see the path running along it. Feeling confident that you know where to go, you turn right. Soon you arrive at the inn.

You enter the inn and immediately feel its warmth. You see a comfortable chair waiting for you in the front room. You sink down into this chair, heave a sigh of relief, and relax. You close your eyes and hear a self-assured voice saying, *"Take the time to rise above where you are and take a good look at where you want to go."* Enjoy the peace of mind that these words bring you.

Take as much time as you need and whenever you're ready, slowly open your eyes. Take time to absorb the meaning of your visualization before you move on to the next section.

Enhancing Your Thinking Skills

Say Goodbye to the Superman/Superwoman Myth.

Don't aim for having it all: a super-charged career, a superb spouse, a sensational sex life, a showcase home, incredible kids, fab vacations, taut body and more. You simply can't have it all—not at the same time anyway. No one can. So make day-by-day choices about the best use of your time and energy. If you notice you're neglecting any aspect of your life for too long, readjust your priorities.

Not only can't you have it all, you also can't *do* it all. Not all by yourself anyway. So, experiment with working in groups. Request assistance from others. Ask colleagues how they're handling a project.

Seek input from family members about family conflict. Involving others expands your resources so that you don't need to do everything by yourself. As a pleaser, you're there for others. Let others be there for you too.

Reduce Your Need for Approval from Others.

If you find yourself living your life to please others or chasing pursuits just to gain acceptance, stop. Though you may initially feel warm and fuzzy as you win another's favor, reflect on whether it's worth it in the long run. If you do say "yes" to what someone else wants, make sure what you do fits into your time schedule and is, at least partially, on your terms.

Nix the guilt if you didn't do what someone else wanted you to do. Nix the fear of offending others. In no way am I suggesting that you become a self-centered, egotistical person. Being a generous, giving person is an admirable quality. But accommodating others just to win their approval or to prove your worthiness is another matter.

Create a Viable Balance between Your Wants and Needs

A well-balanced life is one that has good balance between work and play, tending to today's tasks and preparing for tomorrow's, meeting your needs and meeting the needs of others. Hence, be cognizant of how you spend your time.

Lucky for you, these categories often overlap. Isn't it great when work feels like play? And doing for others feels like you're benefiting too? Still, making a mental distinction between the two will ensure that you don't spend excessive time on another's agenda, minimal time on your own. Aim toward viewing time as your cooperative partner (i.e. I can have fun and still take care of my obligations), not as your challenging opponent (i.e. I never have enough time for me).

To-Do Exercise

Answer these questions:

- Am I maintaining a good balance between what I *want* to do and *need* to do?

- Am I maintaining a good balance between *doing for others* and *doing for myself?*

- What do I spend *too much time* doing?

- What do I spend *insufficient time* doing?

- What steps could I take to make me *feel more in control of my time?*

The answers to these questions will put you on the path to a better balanced life. The ideal situation, of course, is when what you *want* to do and what you *need* to do are one and the same. See how frequently you can make this happen.

> "People often say that a person has not yet found himself. But the self is not something that one finds, It is something that one creates."
>
> ~ **Thomas Szasz**

Make More Active Choices.

Day-to-day pressures easily become overwhelming when you assume that you have no choice in what you're doing, Shy away from a victim, "poor-me" orientation. Instead, view yourself as the one who's in charge of your life. Do this by recognizing that *you* are the one who:

- *Decides* what's important to you

- *Creates* structure to your day

- *Balances* your priorities

- *Maintains* your relationships

- *Manages* your time.

Yes, you need to work within the contingencies of a situation. And yes, it's true that you're not in control of *everything*. But that doesn't mean that you're not in control of *anything*. Know where your power lies and utilize it.

View Life as a Journey, not a Struggle.

To avoid staying stuck in the pleaser-overdoer trap, remind yourself that there's a lot more to life than work. Ask yourself the question: "If I only had one more year to live, what changes would I make to ensure that my time is both enjoyable and productive?" Then see if you can make those changes *now*. Don't immediately say, "I can't." Yes, some changes may not be possible, but some of them will be.

As you take the time to reflect on your life, you may recognize that something doesn't feel right. Hone in on this thought. Ask yourself; "what's missing, what's wrong, what am I neglecting?" In our fast-paced digital age, the answer to these questions often revolves around matters of the heart, spirit and soul. Create at least one change in your daily routine that will provide you with what's missing.

Enriching Your Speaking Skills

Know *when* and *how* to say "no."

The ability to say "no," especially when you're thinking "no," will reap unexpected benefits. Here are just a few:

- It helps you set reasonable limits on your time and energy.

- It helps you build character. Character is weakened by saying "yes" to everyone and everything.

- It helps you gain more respect from others (those who can't say "no" are often treated as doormats).

Here are several ways to say "no."

- A polite "no"—"No, but thanks for thinking of me."

- A "no" with an explanation—"No, I'd like to join you but I have a conflicting engagement."

- A "no" with an alternative proposal—"No, I can't drive you now but I'll have time tomorrow."

- A blunt "no"—"No, I won't do it." As a pleaser, you'll probably use this type of "no" sparingly, saving it for those who ignore more polite forms of "no."

Grant yourself the freedom to use whatever type of "no" best fits your mood and situation.

To-Do Exercise

Recall a situation in which you know you'd have been better off saying "no" but somehow got sucked into saying "yes." If you were in that same situation again, how would you handle it? Think of the exact words you would use. Write down those words. Tuck them in your wallet and look at them every so often. Guaranteed a similar situation will arise and this time you'll be prepared.

Speak More about Your Options, Less about Your Obligations.

Consistently speaking about all you *have to* do without any mention about how you can structure your responsibilities differently will leave you feeling overwhelmed and overburdened. An example: Let's suppose that you're contemplating taking a position as a coach on a kid's soccer team. You'd like to take advantage of the opportunity but you're also worried about whether you'd be overextending yourself. How do you approach such a dilemma?

If you simply view this new opportunity as a burden, you'll be moaning and groaning; one more obligation on your plate—sigh! Focus on your options, however, and the situation appears brighter. You can do this by:

- *Asking* how much time the position will take

- *Making* a pro-con list for yourself

- *Negotiating* your responsibilities

- *Sharing* the work load with another coach

- *Creating* a later start date when time will free up for you

Replace "I'm Supposed to" with "I Want to."

Pleasers typically express themselves by speaking about what they're *supposed to do* (translation: what others *want* them to do). This habit reinforces passivity—both in your own mind and in the minds of your listeners.

Instead of continuing with this type of communication, speak as though you're in charge of your own destiny. For example, instead of saying, "I'm *supposed* to get back to work now," say, "I enjoyed our chat but I *want* to get back to work now." Do you hear the difference between the two sentences? As you take responsibility for what you're doing, you won't be so driven by the need to please. The upshot: greater self-confidence, increased faith in yourself.

Speak More Enthusiastically about Downtime.

It's easy to feel overwhelmed when you've taken on too many responsibilities. Give yourself a break. Take time off. Don't be on the defensive when you're not busily engaged in a productive task. If you hear yourself thinking, "I didn't get a damn thing done the whole weekend," stop. No need to berate yourself. You're entitled to downtime.

Practice making positive comments about non-working times, such as:

- "I spent a fun weekend with friends."

- "It feels great not having anything to do."

- "What a relaxing day!"

End Your Sentences on an Upbeat Note.

Ending your sentences on a downbeat note can make you feel powerless. Make sure that offhand remarks like the ones below don't turn into self-fulfilling prophesies.

- "I have no choice."

- "I'm swamped with work."

- "This pace is killing me."

- "There's nothing I can do about it."

Even if there's an element of truth to these statements, you can still end your thought on an upbeat note by adding a positive clause. Here are the above sentences modified just a bit:

- "I have no choice about taking an in-service program but I can choose a convenient time."

- "I'm swamped with work but I'll finally complete it by the end of the weekend."

- "This pace is killing me but next week a temp will be here to lighten my load."

- "There's nothing I can do about it now but it's taught me an important lesson."

Do you hear how the heart and soul of your communication changes when you end your sentence on an upbeat note? If you speak about yourself as a resilient person who can deal well with difficult situations, don't be surprised if you find yourself evolving into just that kind of person.

> *"Thinking too well of people often allows them to be better than they otherwise would."*
> ~ **Nelson Mandela**

Expanding Your Action Skills

Be More Proactive, Less Reactive.

Seizing the initiative *before* trouble occurs is acting proactively. Taking action only *after* trouble occurs is responding reactively. Paying your estimated taxes on time is proactive; waiting until the IRS is after you is reactive. Looking for a new job before your company crashes is proactive; waiting till you get the ax is reactive. There are some situations in which you don't have the control, yet you can still be proactive. How? Sometimes the answer is easy.

I taught college level psych courses for several years. Since I believe that you'll learn more if you have intrinsic interest in a topic, I gave my students lots of leeway for their term paper. My instructions were simple:

> *"Using at least 3 resources, write a 1500 word paper on any topic relating to human behavior that piques your interest. Imagine that you are the professor and I am the student. When I read your paper, make sure I learn something of interest."*

Naively, I thought my students would be delighted with such an open-ended assignment. A few were. For many, however, this freedom only stirred up their pleasing anxiety:

- "But what do *you want* me to write about?"

- "But what type of resources do *you want* me to use?"

- "But how will *you grade* my paper?"

I had clearly not offered them the structure they were used to receiving. They plaintively cried out, "Tell me what to do." They were unaccustomed to being proactive; hence, they were uncomfortable with the concept. Even if it's been many years since your college days, the above example may hit home. Are you still someone who keeps looking for direction outside of yourself? Do you practically beg others to tell you what to do? If so, it's time to make a change now.

To-Do Exercise

Be proactive at work. Can you suggest a better approach to doing your job? Can you initiate a suggestion box and be the first to contribute to it? If there's no room for proactive people in your company, can you research companies that appreciate such thinking?

Be proactive at home. Can you structure household chores proactively, so that they're not so onerous for you? Can you suggest better ways to share tasks? Can you initiate a family powwow to discuss issues that are bothering you?

Be proactive with your interests. Can you create time to indulge in your interests and hobbies? Can you re-structure your schedule so that every day you savor something special? Can you make sure you set aside time for a vacation at least twice a year?

Give serious thought to these questions. Though you may not be able to implement everything right away, once you're on a proactive path, you'll be surprised at how much you can do that feels empowering.

Practice Basic Time Management Principles.

Ever notice that some people are much more efficient in their use of time than others? Here's a secret to enhancing your time efficiency. Learn to:

Eliminate—Eliminate doing what you don't really need or want to do. Alternatively, make these tasks less frequent. Do you really need to visit your social media networks as often as you do? Or open every e-mail you receive? Or download every app that looks interesting? Reflect on what's important to you. Don't do what everyone else is doing just to fit in.

Delegate—Delegate and/or share the work. If your space is a mess and you're not the only one responsible for it, make sure you're not the only one cleaning it up. As a pleaser, you may be the one that others have been delegating responsibilities to. Now it's time to even up the score. If you're unsure about what to say, return to the speaking skills section—especially the part on "Know when and how to say "no."

Consolidate—You will be a lot more efficient if you consolidate several actions into one. Planning ahead means you combine two shopping trips into one, two chauffeuring trips into one, two e-mail responses into one. Be proactive in scheduling your day. Then *enjoy* the extra time you have for yourself instead of scheduling in one more chore to do.

Hire—Pleasers are often resistant to hiring help; that's one way they get to be juggling so many balls in the air. Of course, having difficulty affording hired help is a factor. However, that excuse is used too readily. If you're totally overwhelmed, it might be that you can't afford *not* to hire someone. Another alternative: consider bartering services. Can you barter accounting services for computer services? Babysitting for shopping trips? Think creatively and a solution may be staring you in the face.

Create Contingency Plans and Backup Systems.

Stuff happens. Plans go awry. Traffic delays you. The unexpected materializes. What are you going to do? It helps if you think about these things beforehand. Is there a neighbor who can pick up your child if you're delayed? If your car is on the blink, do you know an alternative route to work? Think about what might happen and create backup systems *before* an emergency strikes.

Contingency plans don't always involve the assistance of others. Sometimes, it means having what you need in your home before the unexpected happens. Do you have a stock of microwavable dinners in your freezer for when you've no time to cook and don't wish to order in? Do you have a flashlight, batteries and candles on hand for when the next blackout occurs? Do you have an ink refill ready for your printer *before* the ink runs out? Do you have basic first aid material in your medicine cabinet? Think about the last time something unexpected happened. What do you wish you had available at that time? Do you now have it in place or are you naively assuming that nothing like that will happen again anytime soon?

Let Yourself Be.

You are a human being; not a human doing. The busier you are the more important it is for you to have time off to just let yourself be. Pleaser personalities often find that they have no time for simple pleasures. Don't let that happen to you. Here are three activities that you may be giving short shrift to:

- Maintaining friendships

- Engaging in cultural events

- Participating in recreational activities

To-Do Exercise

I started you off with three activities that are not chores, not tasks, not responsibilities. Add at least three other activities to my list that you'd enjoy experiencing, yet typically don't make time for. Why am I emphasizing *this* point in *this* chapter? Because you're a pleaser, I want to make sure that one of the people you're habitually pleasing is—*you*. Because you're an overdoer, I want to make sure that your schedule is not composed primarily of laborious activities. I want you to be excited and energized by life. I hope you want that for yourself as well.

> "The purpose of life, after all, is to live it, to taste experience to the utmost, to reach out eagerly and without fear for newer and richer experiences."
>
> ~ **Eleanor Roosevelt**

Ending Exercise

Congratulations Pleasers! You've completed this chapter. Now take a moment to simply relax and breathe easily. There's so much valuable information in each section. Although you can read it all, you can't absorb it all—not right away. So, review the change program and choose 1, 2, or 3 skills that you want to implement this week. Once you've gotten those under your belt, then you can go back for more. This program is designed to be a *reference* for you. Take in what you can use now. Then when you're ready to incorporate more skills, return to the program and see what's next for you.

Focus on Your *Own* Goals
then
Applaud Your Achievements!

CHAPTER 9

MAKING CHANGE HAPPEN

"Change comes about by having the vision for yourself, believing in yourself, working to get something that you say is important."
~ OPRAH WINFREY

CHANGING INGRAINED PATTERNS IS TOUGH. Sure, you wish it could be easier. You're impatient with yourself; others are impatient with you. They exclaim, "Just do it! Just get it done!" Oh, how I hate the word *"just"* when it pertains to change. We don't change *"just"* because someone wants us to—even ourselves.

Be careful, however, that you don't swing the pendulum in the opposite direction. Chase away those demons that tell you, you can't change: it's too hard, it's not in your DNA, you're too old, you're too rigid, you're too _____ (fill in the blank). Such a mindset will sabotage your efforts before you even begin. Though it's true that "you are who you are," that your personality structure "is what it is," and that the "digital age makes it harder to stay on track," it's also true that you can modify, alter, and tweak your ways so that you become more empowered. And when you do, you will develop a finer version of yourself. Anyone against that?

When you reflect on change as an opportunity to grow (not as an unwanted albatross), then amazing things can happen. I like Muhammad Ali's take on it when he said:

> *"A man who views the world the same at fifty as he did at twenty has wasted thirty years of his life."*

It may be many years until you turn fifty or you may be well beyond fifty. Either way, I hope you don't let rigidity or pessimism stifle your growth. I hope that you flourish and prosper. And that your procrastination pattern becomes a thing of the past. The fact that you've stayed with me this far indicates that you're already on the path to a brighter future. It's hard to imagine that once exposed to the skills and strategies in this book, *something* doesn't take hold.

> "One's mind, once stretched by a new idea, never regains its original dimensions."
> ~ **Oliver Wendell Holmes, Sr.**

Know that change need not be massive to be significant. Moderate change can reap considerable benefits. And a small change in one part of a system can yield gargantuan changes over time; this is what's called the butterfly effect. And here's the best news of all. The payoff for kicking your procrastination pattern will *not* be limited to one area of your life.

It will
Enhance your career,
Enrich your relationships,
Empower your confidence,
Expand your personal well-being.
Wow, What a Payoff!

How Change Happens

Change is a process that takes place over time and typically follows a pattern. Author Anaïs Nin expressed it well when she said:

"There are very few human beings who receive the truth by instant illumination. Most of them acquire it fragment by fragment, on a small scale, by successive developments like a laborious mosaic."

Here now are the typical stages of change.

Awakening

If you're living your life in a daze, unaware of how and when you procrastinate, meaningful change won't happen. This may seem obvious, but it's not to everyone. Lots of people are in denial. Their take on the matter:

- What problem?—It's *your* problem.—Leave me alone!

- Stop picking on me!—Why does this always happen to me?

For some, denial is a deliberate means of avoiding responsibility. For others, it's a genuine lack of self-awareness. Either way, a key aspect of denial is attributing your troubles to others, not to yourself. You may be in denial when:

- You admit that you procrastinate but laugh it off.

- You project the problem onto *someone* else: "They don't understand; they're being unfair; they won't let me be!"

- You project the problem onto *something* else: "Lousy luck; conspiring circumstances; wretched timing."

- You flirt with owning up to your problem but it's just a passing urge in response to someone being upset with you.

Awakening is a prerequisite for change but it's only the first step. What's next?

Awareness

In this stage, you're aware of your procrastination pattern. You've adopted new skills and strategies that you hope will curb your tendency to put things off. You've done much to be proud of. Yet awareness is not the final answer. Why not? Blame it on your brain that bombards you with competing messages. The executive part of your brain wants you to buckle down and do what needs to be done; then the emotional part of your brain pipes in to gummy up the works. Here are two ways this happens:

Brain Rivalry

The executive part and the emotional part of your brain both want to be head honcho. Who wins out? If your emotional self always wins out, you've got problems. No wonder you're behind in your work. But if your executive self wins out, you've also got problems. You don't want to become Mr. Spock, that icon of rationality, do you? Your goal is to ensure that both parts of your brain work cooperatively and that each one has sufficient time in the sun. If you can do this, you will take a quantum leap forward in action, ability and agility. And that's just the A's.

But Excuses

But excuses provide you with a never-ending onslaught of reasons to undermine your intentions. But I'm too tired, but I'm too busy, but I forgot, but, but, but, but…. So you've got to figure out a way to outfox your buts. To refresh your memory, the most important thing you need to know about "but" is that:

Whatever comes *after* the "But" is what counts.
Whatever comes *before* the "But" is simply the excuse.

No-Nonsense Commitment

You're aware of your brain rivalry. You're aware of your But excuses. Now isn't *that* enough? No! Here's why. Let's say you've spent the last six months pigging out on pizza and fries. You've *awakened* to the fact that you no longer fit into your jeans. You're *aware* of why you eat all that high caloric food (it's delicious). Is that enough to get you to buckle down and lose those extra pounds? Rarely. What's missing? A genuine no-nonsense commitment to change. Going on a diet for ten days doesn't do it. Even adding exercise to the mix doesn't do it. Why not? Because if it's not long-term, it's not genuine. It's easy to say you're going to change when you're fed up with your behavior. It's another thing to make a long-term, no-nonsense commitment to change. My definition of such a commitment:

In your quiet moment of truth—when you're alone and not under pressure by anything or anyone—you—your executive self in harmony with your emotional self—make a solemn pledge to change your ways.

No more self-defeating behavior. No more magical thinking. You know it won't be easy, but so what? You're committed to the goal. You acknowledge the need for self-discipline, perseverance, and hard work. You know *why* you want to change. You know *who* you want to be. You know *the life* you want to live. You know that in order to make it happen, your actions must adhere to your beliefs. You have a clear vision in your mind. You have true love in your heart. You have a strong will to do whatever it takes. You know it makes no sense to claim that you want to change but you don't back it up with action. You're tired of disappointing yourself; you're fed up with feeling frustrated. You've learned the skills; you've learned the strategies. Armed with this knowledge, you're ready to:

Get off your butt

Get off your But

MAKE IT HAPPEN!

When the student is ready, the master will appear. This is not only Zen philosophy; this is appreciating the power of the committed mind.

It's Still A Bumpy Road

You're awake, you're aware, you're committed to the need for change. No problem now, right? Wish I could say that's true. But the truth is that there's still a bumpy road ahead of you that might derail your progress. But you didn't come this far to fail. Forewarned is forearmed. So, here's what to watch out for:

Regrets—Coulda, Woulda, Shoulda

Instead of wasting your energy regretting what you didn't do in the past, focus on living up to today's commitments. An example: a graduate student who regrets a stretched-out dissertation may obsess over her lost opportunity. "If only I didn't procrastinate, I could have completed my work before my advisor retired." Yes, that would have been a good idea. But the past is the past. By continuing to focus on her regrets, she avoids doing what she could do *now* to complete her dissertation. Finding a new advisor needs to be her #1 priority.

Here are three constructive ways to deal with regrets:

Learn from them—Regrets can be helpful *if* you learn from them. An example: if you regret that your presentation wasn't well organized because you neglected to create an outline, outline it the next time around. This may seem like an obvious strategy but for many, it's not. Rigidity may result in doing a task the same old way—even when that way doesn't bring the desired results. My personal philosophy: making a *new* mistake is preferable to repeating an old one.

Use regrets as a call to do better—Let your regret be a catalyst for change: *"I'll do better next time."* Or a competitive rallying cry: *"I'll show him."* Avoid using regret as a reason to give up: *"My family never backed me."* Or as a reason to beat yourself up: *"I can't believe I was so dumb."*

Anticipate future regrets before you make new decisions—Give advanced thought to what could go wrong instead of simply acting on impulse. Then, decide on a course of action that could prevent or mitigate future regrets. For example: if you're thinking of not attending a meeting (hopefully for a good reason), contact a colleague in advance who'd be willing to review important content with you.

Here's how Nancy, *a dreamer personality*, used her regrets to prod herself into re-enrolling in design school at age thirty. "I dropped out of design school at age 19 and I've regretted it ever since. I got so tired of hearing myself complain about my stupid decision that I decided to do something about it. But first, I had to stop faulting my parents for not making me stay in school. Oprah writes a column called, *'One Thing I Know For Sure.'* For me, that one thing is that I've got talent. But I also know if I don't develop that talent, my dreams will never see the light of day."

Guilt—Healthy or Neurotic?

Healthy guilt prods you into doing what you know is right. If you want to spend more time with your kids, yet your work keeps beckoning you, healthy guilt will motivate you to create time for both. If you know you need to focus on your work but the Internet keeps seducing you, healthy guilt will be your friend.

Neurotic guilt, however, is like the Eveready Bunny. It keeps going and going. No matter what steps you take to curb your procrastination, you feel guilty. No matter what's right in your life, you find something that's wrong. Wallowing in guilt, like nursing regrets, robs you of your energy. Though you recognize the need for change, you don't develop the motivation to move forward.

Here's how Neil, *a defier personality,* transformed his neurotic guilt into healthy guilt. "People think defiers never feel guilty. Not true. We hide a lot. After a mediocre review at work, I'd feel guilty. But did that mean I'd do things differently? No way. I was too busy feeling like a loser. After just two coaching sessions, however, I realized how much I isolate myself at work. Now, I put myself out there, I'm more cooperative and I'm receiving first-rate reviews."

Criticism—Hurtful and Helpful

Especially if you were raised in the era of endless praise, you may wish there were nothing about you to criticize. Whatever you do is fine. Whatever you say is great. Whatever you think is fantastic. But don't kid yourself. It's not true. Listen instead to the words of Winston Churchill:

> *"Criticism may not be agreeable, but it is necessary.*
> *It fulfills the same function as pain in the human body.*
> *It calls attention to an unhealthy state of things."*

Let's turn to *"American Idol"* to see how to use criticism well. Judges on that show critique contestants every move. Sometimes they're kind, other times they're downright insulting. But if you're a contestant, you listen. Why? Because your goal is to improve your performance. Receiving on target, constructive feedback can help you do just that. Even if you receive criticism that's harsh, it can be helpful. If you've given little effort to your work or believe you're a star when you're really a bimbo, you may well deserve harsh feedback. You're wasting everybody's time by not dealing with an undertaking seriously. However, if you've put in the effort yet your performance is still knocked, reframe it as a critique.

A critique is a discriminating review used for works of art and literature. When an editor critiques a journalist's article, she's doing it to *help* the writer get published. When a theater critic critiques a show, he's *helping* the director know what works and what doesn't work. This feedback is invaluable to a show's success. Broadway shows typically open out-of-town to receive a critique *before* their New York opening. By doing so, they have a chance to work out the kinks and be ready for opening night in the Big Apple.

Next time you receive criticism, wanted or unwanted, challenge yourself to see how it might be of value to you. Here's how Samantha, *a pleaser personality,* learned to appreciate criticism: "I was always so afraid of what others would think. Not anymore. I don't let people intimidate me. I've even asked friends to critique my work. I would never have done that before; I was so emotionally fragile. The feedback I've received from friends has been surprisingly valuable."

Getting Back on Track

You're on track. You're in a groove. You're inspired. You're confident. And then you're not. It's over for now.

You're off track. You're in a rut. Your commitment wavers. You've lost your confidence. What happened?

Know that it's the norm, not the exception, to lapse into a rut. Such times may be part of a general slump in your life or a response to a specific situation. Don't give up! Do be prepared, however, to get back on track as soon as you can. View any setback as temporary and:

- *Nix the guilt.* Guilt undermines your ability to bounce back.

- *Nix the shame.* Shame undercuts your worth as a human being.

- *Nix the harsh words.* Encourage yourself with gentle words.

- *Nix the punishment.* Be kind to yourself.

Question everything, if you insist, but don't question your ability to emerge from the rut. Here are a few ideas to help you do just that:

Recall your original intention. Remind yourself what your original goal was. Why were you interested in beating your procrastination pattern when you picked up this book? What was important to you then?

Envision yourself in a better place. Imagine how good it will feel when you accomplish your goal. Visualize building a bridge from rut-land to groove-land. Picture yourself crossing the bridge. It won't be long now 'til you'll be back where you belong.

Visualize a hero of yours. Male or female, alive or dead, real or mythical—it doesn't matter. Heroes come in all forms. Picture your hero cheering you on. What does he say to you? How does he let you know he cares? How does she encourage you? How is she supportive? Soak up her words. Ingest his caring. Keep your hero close by as you go about your day.

View life as a long-distance marathon, not a sprint. Since you're in it for the long haul, don't let the first hint of frustration sabotage your goals. Take time to rest, eat, pray, heal, love. One day the sun will shine. When it does, you'll pick yourself up, dust yourself off and get back on track.

Monitor your momentum. Quantum leaps are not necessary; small steps are fine as long you're moving forward. If you find yourself falling behind, take an action. Change your scenery. Talk to a friendly face. Throw out unneeded stuff. Sit down to a good meal. Do something— anything that gets your energy going.

Use your mind—even when you don't feel like it. You know that working out is the tried and true road to a buff body. Did you know that this is also true for your mind? Don't let those neurons stagnate. Deliberate, meditate, cogitate. Use your mind, not to berate yourself, but to remember and utilize the great skills and strategies you have just learned.

Success

You've arrived! And it feels good! Triumphing over your procrastination has *not* turned you into a no-fun, dreary workaholic as you once feared. Indeed, it's quite the opposite. Life has become easier, not harder; more fun, not less fun. Why should this be so? Terence, a Roman orator, who lived eons before the digital age, provides us with a succinct answer:

> *"There is nothing so easy but it becomes difficult*
> *when you do it reluctantly."*

Wonder how contemporary people view their lives *after* procrastination? Here are a few success stories:

John, *a perfectionist personality*, described his new life: "It's liberating to be a 'regular' person; not always reaching for unattainable goals. It took me forever to realize that my lofty ambitions were hurting me and that I could be successful without needing to be insanely successful. Over-the-top expectations no longer swirl about in my head, making my life one big headache!"

Kathy, *a dreamer personality*, summed it up this way: "Once I got a grip on my time-wasting habits, I found a new group of friends—really positive people. It's as if I made a metamorphosis from a head-in-the-clouds dreamer to a sought-after magnet. People used to view me as flaky; now they see me as down-to-earth. That's better. And I don't feel so phony or lonely anymore."

Melissa, *a worrier personality, said:* "I feel as if I've learned a secret formula for how to deal with anything. No longer do I get so worked up over the great, big, overwhelming chore in front of me. Nowadays, I break the chores into smaller, easier ones that don't send me into a tailspin. Then, one by one, I get it all done."

Jerry, *a crisis-maker personality,* described his newly developed sense of self-worth: "I no longer need to wait till crunch time to get my motor running. Neither do I need to work all night to do what I should have done earlier. My life is saner now. And I feel better about the kind of person I have become."

Shelley, *a defier personality,* confessed: "People find me more agreeable today than they used to. With my procrastination in check, I don't get snide remarks from friends who used to be pissed when I showed up late. I've also stopped bucking heads with authority figures. It's paid off big time with my mentor who has been incredibly valuable to me in my career growth."

Holly, *a pleaser personality,* declared: "I've left behind the world of cliques. I've stopped trying to get others to like me by always doing what they wanted. Once I learned to value my own thoughts, I made a career change. Paying attention to your own ideas might be a no-brainer for others, but for me it's real progress."

A Final Word

Understanding, implementing and reinforcing the skills in this book doesn't happen right away. Be patient with yourself. Give yourself time to make it happen. But do make it happen. Your future is highly dependent on the habits you develop *now.*

> *"Though no one can go back and make a brand new start, anyone can start from now and make a brand new ending."*
> ~ **Carl Bard**

HOW TECHNOLOGY CAN BOOST YOUR PRODUCTIVITY

DOESN'T IT FEEL GREAT when you realize you've made progress toward reaching your goals? Don't you love the confidence you experience when you get things done in a timely way? Now, let's keep that momentum going!

You've put a lot of effort into engaging with this book. And hopefully, it's paid off. You now have a deeper understanding of your personality style. You know how you get seduced into putting things off. And you know how to get yourself out of a procrastination rut. You also recognize how easily technology can suck up your time. But can it also boost your productivity? Yes it can!

Digital technology is what you make of it. It can help you get things done or it can undercut your best intentions. Though the hypnotic allure of the Web will always be a constant, the Web itself may actually help you to resist it. How can it do that? Let me show you the ways.

Blocking Distractions

You're aware that the time you spend playing games, reading blogs, Twittering, Facebooking and aimless surfing robs you of the time you need to achieve your goals. But how do you stop yourself from doing these activities when you're so drawn to them? Do the obvious. Close your e-mail. Shut down your social media sites. Turn off your Web access. Disconnect your cell. Yes, I know this is easier said than done. So, if you need help in removing these distractions, let tech come to the rescue.

There are sites that can function like a nurturing parent—nudging you to get back to business and cheering you on when you achieve your goals. They do this by blocking you from either the entire Internet or specific sites until a predetermined time that you've set. Might a little guilt also help keep you in tow? Try weaseling your way out of your previous commitment and receive a conscience-pricking message like, "shouldn't you be working?" Check out *StayFocusd* (no 'e'), *Leechblock, Lifehacker, and Anti-social* to see if one of them can be your virtual nurturing parent.

Tracking Time

Not sure how well you're utilizing your time? Lose track of where all the hours have gone? Consider using a productivity tracking site, such as *MyHours, yaTimer, ManicTime, RescueTime*. Such programs will tell you exactly where your time goes, tracking every Web page you visit, every application you use, and providing you with time tracking reports and graphs.

To-Do Lists

With so many things to do, it's easy to forget what you were "going to do." So, thank goodness for those ubiquitous yellow sticky pads. Now all you have to do is remember where you put the pad and remember to look at it. If you're forgetful like that, let virtual yellow pads come to the rescue. You can't misplace them and you can't ignore them because they're gadgets that pop up on your home page or on your phone. For more types of virtual reminders to help you manage your tasks and schedule future e-mails, check out *RemembertheMilk. TimeCave, reQuall.*

Taking Notes

Have you noticed how complicated most projects become over time? And surely you're aware that you get busier and busier with stuff to organize, locate and do? Indeed, you've been so busy that the ingenious idea that popped into your head just a few hours ago has popped right out of your head and is now floating around somewhere in outer space. Not good. So, get yourself a cyberspace brain that can remember all your stuff, organize your thoughts and archive your work. Check out *Evernote, Scrivener, and Delicious* to see how they can improve your real memory.

Digital Calendars

If you haven't gone digital with your calendar, check out Microsoft Outlook and Google's iCalendar to see if they can make life easier for you. Your calendar does not need to be complicated to be effective. Indeed, simple is often best. But you do need to write down those time gobblers that you otherwise forget about (i.e. preparation, transportation, organization) in addition to your work and family responsibilities. Otherwise, you'll keep wondering, *where did the day go?*

Using Egg Timers

People still use a simple egg timer. If you're really young, you might be wondering—what's an egg-timer? Before stoves had built-in timers, you had to keep track of the time to get your boiled egg cooked the way you liked it. Nowadays people set egg timers for everything except eggs. To use a virtual egg timer and other count-down timers, go to *e.ggtimer* or *online-stopwatch*. Set your timer, then work or play until you hear your digital ding—the signal to wrap it up and move on.

Online Bookmarks

"Not now, later." This is the rhetoric that gets so many procrastinators in trouble. Yet there are times that those words are spot-on. Let's assume that you're engrossed in an important project. Yet, your wandering eye lands on a breaking story or enticing link. Don't break your concentration. You'll only feel scattered and upset with yourself. Instead, *bookmark* the site on your computer and go to it later.

Moving Forward

Remember your goals. You're ready! You're primed! You no longer want to be held back by your old habits! You picked up this book for a reason. I hope you're glad you did.

You've learned much, including:

- Enhanced thinking patterns that create a richer reality

- Persuasive speaking patterns that shape a richer world

- Agile acting patterns that give rise to a richer terrain

And now you've discovered how tech tools (used properly) can help you swim against the current that ceaselessly pulls you backwards into the familiar waters of the past. But you're smarter now. You can envision a wider road ahead that stretches out invitingly. And I have faith that you will put yourself on that road and find your rhythm. When you do, I trust you will dance.

ABOUT THE AUTHOR

Linda Sapadin, Ph.D. is a psychologist and success coach who specializes in helping people enrich their lives, enhance their relationships and overcome self-defeating patterns of behavior.

I'd like to hear from you. Tell me how you're doing and what ideas in this book were most useful to you. **lsapadin@drsapadin.com.**

If you're finding it tough to move ahead on your own, check out my **coaching services** on **www.BeatProcrastinationCoach.com.** Often, just a few sessions can jump-start your progress.

Enjoy learning about psychological and relationship issues? Visit **www.PsychWisdom.com.** Read the many articles archived there. Scroll down the left menu to subscribe to my free bi-monthly newsletter.

CPSIA information can be obtained
at www.ICGtesting.com
Printed in the USA
LVHW051921190723
752771LV00004B/23

9 780983 676652